PEP GUARD.OLA

88 Attacking Combinations and Positional Patterns of Play Direct from Pep's Training Sessions

Published by

PEP GUARDIOLA

88 Attacking Combinations and Positional Patterns of Play Direct from Pep's Training Sessions

First Published July 2019 by SoccerTutor.com
info@soccertutor.com | www.SoccerTutor.com

UK: 0208 1234 007 | **US:** (305) 767 4443 | **ROTW:** +44 208 1234 007
ISBN: 978-1-910491-32-4

Edited by
Alex Fitzgerald - SoccerTutor.com

Cover Design by
Alex Macrides, Think Out Of The Box Ltd.
Email: design@thinkootb.com Tel: +44 (0) 208 144 3550

Diagrams
Diagram designs by SoccerTutor.com. All the diagrams in this book have been created using SoccerTutor.com Tactics Manager Software available from www.SoccerTutor.com

Note: While every effort has been made to ensure the technical accuracy of the content of this book, neither the author nor publishers can accept any responsibility for any injury or loss sustained as a result of the use of this material.

CONTENTS

ATTACKING COMBINATIONS & FINISHING 110

PEP GUARDIOLA ACHIEVEMENTS

COACHING ROLES

- **Manchester City** (2016 - Present)
- **Bayern Munich** (2013 - 2016)
- **Barcelona** (2008 - 2012)
- **Barcelona B** (2007 - 2008)

"When I have the ball, I have a chance to score a goal."

"My football is simple: I like to attack, attack and attack."

"When in doubt, go back to the basics, attack, attack, always attack."

HONOURS **(Europe/World)**

- **UEFA Champions League x 2** (2009, 2011)
- **FIFA Club World Cup x 3** (2009, 2011, 2013)
- **UEFA Super Cup x 3** (2009, 2011, 2013)

HONOURS **(Domestic Leagues)**

- **English Premier League x 2** (2018, 2019)
- **German Bundesliga x 3** (2014, 2015, 2016)
- **Spanish La Liga x 3** (2009, 2010, 2011)
- **Spanish Tercera (2nd) División** (2008)

HONOURS **(Domestic Cups)**

- **English FA Cup** (2019)
- **German DFB-Pokal x 2** (2014, 2016)
- **Spanish Copa del Rey x 2** (2009, 2012)
- **English EFL Cup x 2** (2018, 2019)
- **Spanish Supercopa de España x 3** (2009, 2010, 2011)

INDIVIDUAL AWARDS

- **FIFA World Coach of the Year** (2011)
- **European Coach of Season - Press Association** (2011)
- **European Coach of Year - Alf Ramsey Award** (2009)
- **English Premier League Manager of Season** (2018)
- **La Liga Coach of the Year x 4** (2009, 2010, 2011, 2012)

PEP GUARDIOLA: BEST QUOTES FROM PLAYERS

"I had a unique master. I grew a lot with Pep as a player and learnt a great deal from him. Some managers are superb tacticians, but Pep would also describe the moves you had to make on the pitch and what would happen then. And it did!" (Lionel Messi)

"He is a genius who reads the game and covers every situation imaginable. He is always showing us how to create space and find solutions and there is no manager like him, which makes him probably the best in the world." (Ilkay Gündoğan)

"There is one thing you can be sure of — he wants to dominate. People associate his teams with the number of goals they score but his teams also don't concede a lot. He always wants to be on the front foot, having the ball, possession, and he wants to dominate." (Thierry Henry)

"I have learned a lot from Pep. He's a genius. I can learn more from him in an hour than from others in one year. He not only lifts you to the next level on the pitch, but also in your mind. He has revealed totally new options to me. I did not know that was possible when I got to Munich. He found a new position for me." (Douglas Costa)

"He is an incredible coach on a completely different level in terms of tactics. He really helps players develop and he even helped me improve at the age of 30." (Phillip Lahm)

DIAGRAM KEY

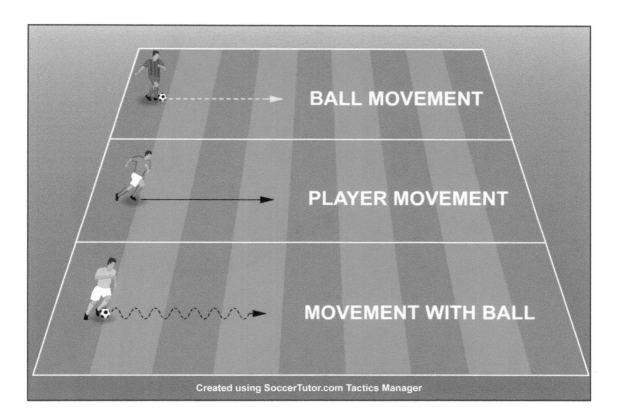

BALL MOVEMENT

PLAYER MOVEMENT

MOVEMENT WITH BALL

Created using SoccerTutor.com Tactics Manager

PRACTICE FORMAT

- The practices in this book are direct from Pep Guardiola's training sessions at Manchester City, Bayern Munich and FC Barcelona.

- Each attacking combination or attacking positional pattern of play includes the practice topic/name and clear diagrams with a detailed description.

PEP GUARDIOLA'S POSITIONAL PATTERNS OF PLAY TRAINING

PEP GUARDIOLA'S ATTACKING PHILOSOPHY: BEST QUOTES

"You can lose balls and face counter attacks. But I think it is more risk when you don't risk."

"It's impossible against a deep defence to be narrow. First be wide and then after that, runs in behind."

"I try to move a well organised defensive opponent - move them, so the pass of the ball is quick and creates problems in the defensive structures."

"Sometimes there are teams high pressing and you find the spaces sometimes easier - you have more space, and the other ones who defend deep with 11 players in the box, OK, you have to find a way to attack them."

"I love to attack, That's my idea of football. It is the speed of the attack that will intrigue."

"The important thing is the intentions. I try to take the ball, to try to play, to try to attack. After that, win or don't win."

"While we attack, the idea is to always keep your position, always being in the place you have to be."

" I want dynamism, mobility, but the position has always got to be filled by someone."

Source: Pep Guardiola Interview with Transversales on SFR Sport 1, France - February 2018

PEP GUARDIOLA'S ATTACKING PHILOSOPHY: KEY ASPECTS

Never drop out of position to come looking for the ball

Use passing combination play to move your opponents out of position

Wingers high up and wide at the edge of the pitch, waiting to strike clinically when the opposition is disorganised

Dominate the game high up the pitch

Possession is just a tool

Create 1v1 situations in key areas

Structured positioning of the players - gradually move up pitch together

Correct body shape to receive the ball

Short accurate passes

Use a "Third Man" when building up play between the lines of the opposition
(create a free man with passing triangles)

2 v 4 in attack, extra man in midfield, extra man in defence, with a high defensive line

Play with 'intensity' and total concentration for the duration of every game

Source: Perarnau, Martí. Pep Guardiola: The Evolution . Birlinn. Kindle Edition, 2016

PEP GUARDIOLA'S POSITIONAL PLAY (JUEGO DE POSICIÓN)

Exploit space in possession and cover space out of possession

Passing options are predetermined by the position of the ball and players shift according to the position of the ball

Keep the correct distances between each other in relation to the players' positioning and the pattern of play

Controlled possession

Players are positioned within specific zones

Move the opposition's defence

Create gaps and passing lanes (triangles)

Position players in between the lines

Break through the opposition's lines with forward passing

Play forward to a team-mate in space to progress the move or to a team-mate with enough time and space to receive and then pass again

It is key to take up the correct positions within a defined structure (team organisation)

"Half Spaces" (see next pages) and winning the ball back quickly after losing it are born from Juego de Posición

Source: Luca Bertolini, UEFA B Coaching Licence and Author of many football coaching books - **www.lucamistercalcio.com**

15

PEP GUARDIOLA'S TRAINING PITCH ZONES: KEY AREAS

PEP'S TRAINING PITCH ZONES: Marked out zones on the training pitch to practice specific positional patterns of play, maximise space, disorganise the opposition, create numerical advantages and move the ball into dangerous attacking areas ("Half Spaces").

Attacking Midfielders and the "Half Spaces"

▷ Attacking midfielders aim to receive in this area and turn

▷ From here, the most creative players look to pass in behind

Wide Zones

▷ Wingers stay within higher wide zone (wing backs in 3-5-2 = lower)

▷ They occupy opposing defenders

▷ They make runs in behind in the final stage of the attack

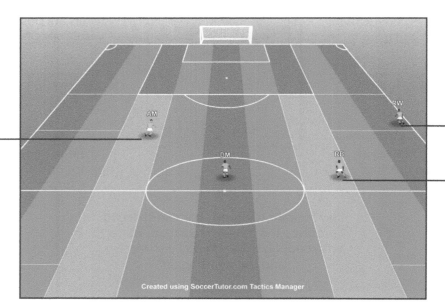

Created using SoccerTutor.com Tactics Manager

Inverted Full Backs and the "Half Spaces"

▷ In Man City's 4-3-3, the inverted full backs are positioned in the "Half Spaces" to help move the ball from the centre backs to the attackers

▷ This allows the defensive midfielder to stay in a central position

16

PEP GUARDIOLA'S TRAINING PITCH ZONES: RULES AND AIMS

Effective possession play, gradual build-up play as a tool to move opposing players and disorganise their defence

Penetrate the opposition effectively and receive between their midfield and defensive lines

After controlled possession, arrive at the penalty area with many players ready to attack a pass in behind or cross

The higher wide zones must always be occupied by the wingers when Pep Guardiola uses the 3-5-2 formation

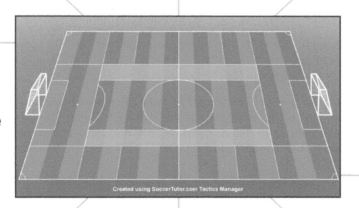

Created using SoccerTutor.com Tactics Manager

The lower wide zones must always be occupied by the wing backs when Pep Guardiola uses the 3-5-2 formation

"Just from you being high and wide, you are actually freezing 4 players because we are threatening to go in behind." (Thierry Henry)

"When you have Xavi, Iniesta, Busquets, Messi, Fabregas, it is normal you play in that position in the middle." (Pep Guardiola)

"When you have players here like Sane, Sterling and De Bruyne, we attack more the spaces." (Pep Guardiola)

17

THE IMPORTANCE OF PEP GUARDIOLA'S "HALF SPACES"

WHAT ARE PEP GUARDIOLA'S "HALF SPACES"?

The "Half Spaces" are the inside channels between the opposing full back and centre back on either side of the area (see diagram on the next page). Pep Guardiola's aim is to have his best and most creative players receive inside these "Half Spaces."

- Currently at Manchester City, Pep Guardiola wants his attacking midfielders **Silva (21)**, **De Bruyne (17)** and **Bernado (20)** to receive the ball in the "Half Space" high up the pitch. From there, they look to play a pass in behind the defensive line.

- Manchester City try to make sure they have a numerical advantage in the middle third with the inverted full backs **Walker (2)** and **Zinchenko (35)** or **Delph (18)** taking up central positions, creating a 2-3-2-3 attacking formation (see page 28).

- The inverted full backs (4-3-3) are positioned within the "Half Spaces" and help move the ball from the centre backs to the attackers, as well as allowing the defensive midfielder **Fernandinho (25)** to maintain a central position.

- Pep Guardiola's wingers **Sterling (7)**, **Sané (19)**, **Mahrez (26)** and sometimes **Bernado (20)** play in the higher wide zone at the edge of the pitch. This forces the opposing full backs to stay back and creates more space in the centre and in the "Half Spaces" for their team-mates to receive and exploit.

- At Bayern Munich, Pep Guardiola wanted his wingers (or wide forwards) **Robben** and **Ribery** to receive the ball in the "Half Spaces" high up the pitch, cut inside and shoot. This was because they were the most dangerous players.

- This meant that the full backs or wing backs stayed in the wide zones to leave the space in the "Half Space."

- At FC Barcelona, Pep Guardiola wanted his attacking midfielders **Xavi** and **Iniesta** to receive the ball in the "Half Spaces" high up the pitch.

- The wingers would stay wide to occupy the defenders and leave the "Half Spaces" open for **Xavi** and **Iniesta** to receive and then play a pass in behind the defensive line.

Source: Luca Bertolini, UEFA B Coaching Licence and Author of many football coaching books - **www.lucamistercalcio.com**

PEP GUARDIOLA'S "HALF SPACES" EXAMPLE: MAN CITY (4-3-3)

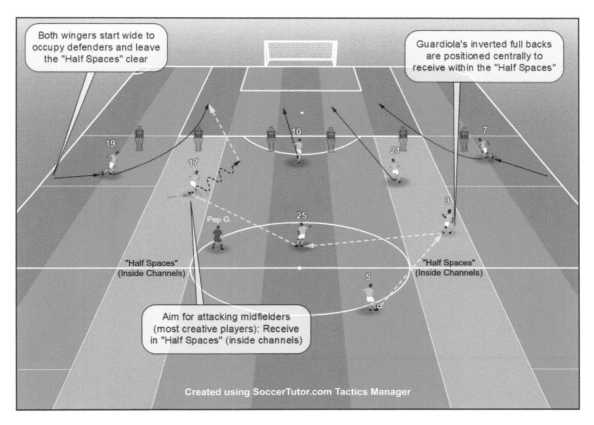

Both wingers start wide to occupy defenders and leave the "Half Spaces" clear

Guardiola's inverted full backs are positioned centrally to receive within the "Half Spaces"

"Half Spaces" (Inside Channels)

"Half Spaces" (Inside Channels)

Aim for attacking midfielders (most creative players): Receive in "Half Spaces" (inside channels)

Created using SoccerTutor.com Tactics Manager

- Manchester City are using the 4-3-3 formation with their inverted full backs positioned within the "Half Spaces" to help move the ball from the centre backs to the attacking players.

- If the Manchester City attacking midfielders receive unmarked within the "Half Spaces" and are able to turn, they then try to play a pass in behind the defensive line.

- Both wingers **(19 & 7)** start in wide positions near to the touchline to occupy the opposing defenders and make sure there is space for their team-mates (attacking midfielders) to receive within the "Half Space."

- In this example, the defensive midfielder **Fernandinho (25)** receives from the inverted right back **Sagna (3)** and passes to the attacking midfielder **De Bruyne (17)** within the "Half Space."

- From this point, **De Bruyne (17)** has many options to play a pass in behind.

19

ATTACKING POSITIONAL PATTERNS OF PLAY (4-3-3)

Building Up Play from the GK Practice Example

Direct from
Pep Guardiola's
Bayern Munich
Training Session

Building Up Play from the GK Practice Example: 3v3 Situation Out Wide

The practices to follow in this section show Pep Guardiola's positional patterns of play to attack in the opposition half. Most of the time, Pep's teams face an opposition defending deep in their own half, so these patterns are very useful to find attacking solutions to create chances and score goals.

Here we show a practice example from Pep Guardiola's training session with Bayern Munich in 2015, where the players practice building up play from deep in their own half from a goal kick.

Example A: Pass to FB Blocked and DM Closely Marked

Created using SoccerTutor.com Tactics Manager

Description (Example A)

The GK passes to the centre back (**CB**), who dribbles forward.

The opposing winger blocks the pass to the full back (**FB**) and the defensive midfielder (**DM**) is closely marked.

The winger (**W**) drops back to provide a passing option and brings his marker with him.

The centre back (**CB**) passes to the winger (**W**), who plays a first time pass to the full back (**FB**). The full back (**FB**) runs forward to receive and dribble into the space created.

Source: Pep Guardiola's Bayern Munich training session in Doha, Qatar - 17th January 2015

22

Example B: Pass to DM Blocked and FB Closely Marked

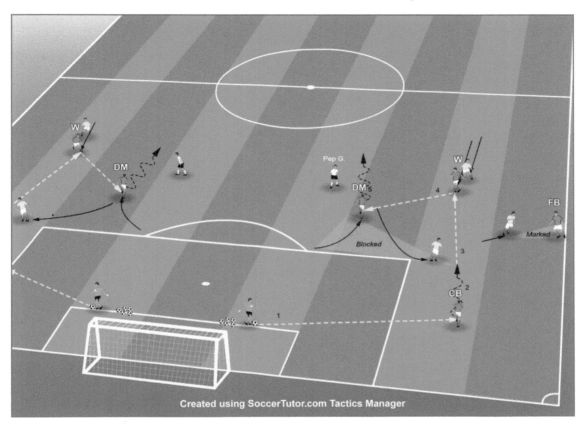

Created using SoccerTutor.com Tactics Manager

Description (Example B)

In this variation, the pass to the defensive midfielder (**DM**) is blocked and the full back (**FB**) is closely marked.

The winger (**W**) again drops back to provide a passing option and brings his marker with him.

The centre back (**CB**) passes to the winger (**W**), who this time plays a first time pass inside to the defensive midfielder (**DM**).

The defensive midfielder (**DM**) runs forward to receive and dribble forward into the space.

Source: Pep Guardiola's Bayern Munich training session in Doha, Qatar - 17th January 2015

23

Example C: Pass to Winger Blocked and DM Closely Marked

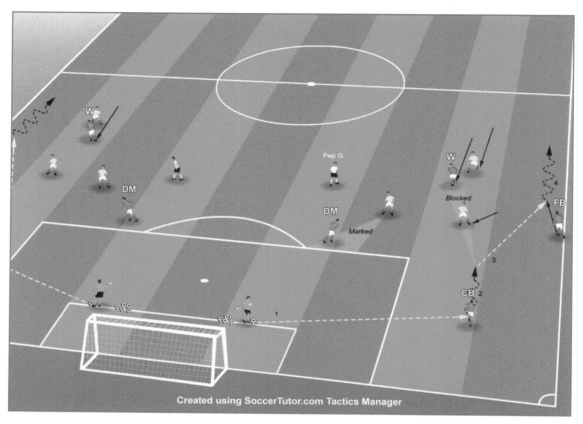

Created using SoccerTutor.com Tactics Manager

Description (Example C)

In this variation, the defensive midfielder (**DM**) is closely marked.

The winger (**W**) again drops back to provide a passing option and brings his marker with him, but the opposing winger moves across to block the pass.

Therefore, the centre back (**CB**) passes out wide to the full back (**FB**), who is free to receive and dribble forward into the space created.

Source: Pep Guardiola's Bayern Munich training session in Doha, Qatar - 17th January 2015

Attacking Positional Patterns of Play: 4-3-3 with Inverted Full Backs

Direct from
Pep Guardiola's
Manchester City
Training Session

"What I love most is those who claim that you couldn't play like this in Germany or the Premier League, with Silva, Bernardo, Agüero, all of whom are 5 foot tall. But we've done it. By receiving few goals and dominating the game through positional play."

Source: Pep Guardiola Interview by Antoni Bassas for Daily ARA - Published on July 5th 2019

MANCHESTER CITY'S 4-3-3 FORMATION

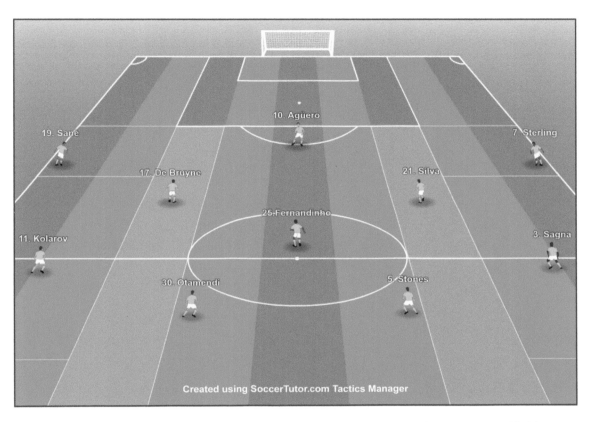

Created using SoccerTutor.com Tactics Manager

- **30. Otamendi:** Left Centre Back
- **5. Stones:** Right Centre Back
- **11. Kolarov:** Left Back
- **3. Sagna:** Right Back
- **25. Fernandinho:** Defensive Midfielder

- **17. De Bruyne:** Left Attacking Midfielder
- **21. Silva:** Right Attacking Midfielder
- **19. Sané:** Left Winger
- **7. Sterling:** Right Winger
- **10. Agüero:** Forward

Source: Pep Guardiola's Manchester City training session at Etihad Campus Training Ground, Manchester - 12th July 2017

MANCHESTER CITY'S 2-3-2-3 ATTACKING FORMATION (4-3-3)

Created using SoccerTutor.com Tactics Manager

- During the attacking phase, Pep Guardiola's Manchester city team change their formation to an attacking 2-3-2-3 shape, which creates 4 lines for the ball to be moved through.

- This allows the full backs to become "Inverted Full Backs" and take up positions more centrally to receive within the "Half Spaces" (see next page for more detail).

- In this 2-3-2-3 formation, the defensive midfielder **Fernadinho (25)** can stay in a central position without the need to cover space to his right or left.

- The 2 wingers **Sterling (7)** and **Sané (19)** stay wide to occupy the opposing defenders and leave space for their team-mates to receive the ball in the centre and "Half Spaces."

- The centre backs **Stones (5)** and **Otamendi (30)** pass to the defensive midfielder or an inverted full back. They then move the ball to the forward or an attacking midfielder.

- The wingers **Sterling (7)** and **Sané (19)** only become active for the final stage of attack and make runs in behind to receive. They either receive and finish or deliver low crosses.

Source: Pep Guardiola's Manchester City training session at Etihad Campus Training Ground, Manchester - 12th July 2017

POSITIONING AND RECEIVING IN THE "HALF SPACES" (4-3-3)

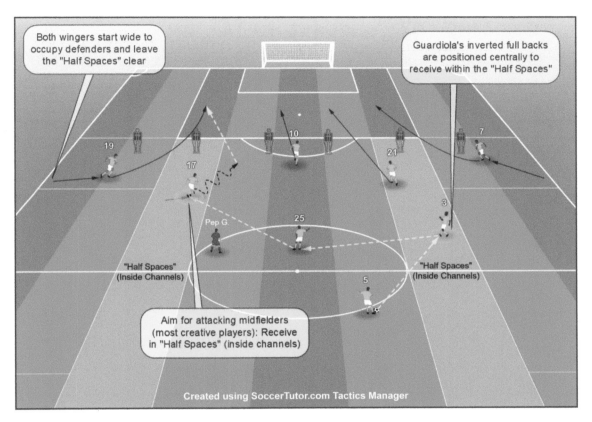

Both wingers start wide to occupy defenders and leave the "Half Spaces" clear

Guardiola's inverted full backs are positioned centrally to receive within the "Half Spaces"

"Half Spaces" (Inside Channels)

"Half Spaces" (Inside Channels)

Aim for attacking midfielders (most creative players): Receive in "Half Spaces" (inside channels)

Created using SoccerTutor.com Tactics Manager

- If the Manchester City attacking midfielders receive unmarked within the "Half Spaces" and are able to turn, they then try to play a final ball in behind.

- Pep Guardiola wants his wingers **(19 & 7)** to stay wide to occupy the defenders and leave space for his attacking midfielders to receive within the "Half Space" and turn unmarked.

- He also wants his inverted full backs - **Sagna (3)** in diagram example - to receive within the "Half pace" and take part in building up play through the lines.

- In this example, Manchester City are using the 4-3-3 formation and the inverted right back **Sagna (3)** passes to the defensive midfielder **Fernandinho (25)**, who passes to the attacking midfielder **De Bruyne (17)** within the "Half Space."

- From this point, **De Bruyne (17)** has options to play a pass in behind. In the diagram example, he dribbles inside and passes in behind for the left winger **Sané (19)** to run onto.

Source: Pep Guardiola's Manchester City training session at Etihad Campus Training Ground, Manchester - 12th July 2017

PEP GUARDIOLA'S TRAINING SET-UP (INVERTED FULL BACKS)

2 players in every position take turns alternately

Created using SoccerTutor.com Tactics Manager

- This diagram shows Pep Guardiola's set-up for practicing attacking positional patterns of play in the 4-3-3 with inverted full backs.

- There are coaches either side with many balls, ready to pass to the centre backs to start the pattern (build up).

- There are also 6 mannequins in a line outside the penalty area, as shown.

- In each position, there are 2 players (1 blue and 1 yellow), which forms 2 teams of 10 outfield players to practice patterns.

- The 2 teams run the patterns outlined by Pep Guardiola alternately. As soon as one team finishes, they jog back to their positions and the next team goes.

Source: Pep Guardiola's Manchester City training session at Etihad Campus Training Ground, Manchester - 12th July 2017

1. Both Attacking Midfielders Combine to Attack Through the Centre

Created using SoccerTutor.com Tactics Manager

Description

1. The right centre back (5) passes to the inverted right back (3).

2. The right back (3) passes inside to the defensive midfielder (25).

3. The defensive midfielder (25) receives and moves forward with the ball.

4. The defensive midfielder (25) plays a diagonal pass to the attacking midfielder (17) in the "Half Space."

5. The attacking midfielder (17) shifts across

slightly and passes to the other attacking midfielder (21) on the move.

6. The second attacking midfielder (21) also moves inside to receive and dribbles forward into the penalty area.

7. The second attacking midfielder (21) tries to score.

8. The forward (10) and both wingers (19 and 7) have made runs into the penalty area and are alert to finish any rebounds.

Source: Pep Guardiola's Manchester City training session at Etihad Campus Training Ground, Manchester - 12th July 2017

2. Attacking Midfielder Moves Inside to Receive Forward's Lay-off and Pass in Behind to the Winger

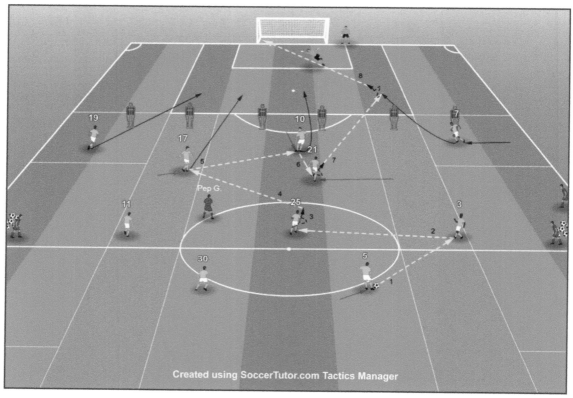

Created using SoccerTutor.com Tactics Manager

Description

1. The right centre back (5) passes to the inverted right back (3).

2. The right back (3) passes inside to the defensive midfielder (25).

3. The defensive midfielder (25) receives and moves forward with the ball.

4. The defensive midfielder (25) plays a diagonal pass to the attacking midfielder (17) in the "Half Space."

5. The attacking midfielder (17) passes to the forward (10) in the centre.

6. The forward (10) lays the ball back to the other attacking midfielder (21), who shifts across into the centre to receive.

7. The second attacking midfielder (21) receives, opens up and plays a diagonal pass in behind to the winger (7).

8. The winger (7) receives and tries to score.

Source: Pep Guardiola's Manchester City training session at Etihad Campus Training Ground, Manchester - 12th July 2017

3. Attacking Midfielder Receives in the "Half Space," Dribbles Inside and Plays in Behind to the Winger

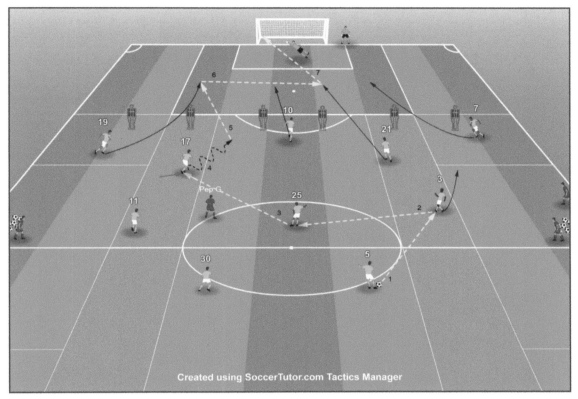

Created using SoccerTutor.com Tactics Manager

Description

1. The right centre back (5) passes to the inverted right back (3).

2. The right back (3) passes inside to the defensive midfielder (25).

3. The defensive midfielder (25) plays a diagonal pass to the attacking midfielder (17) in the "Half Space."

4. The attacking midfielder (17) moves inside and forward with the ball.

5. The attacking midfielder (17) plays a pass in behind for the run of the left winger (19).

6. The winger (19) cuts the ball back for oncoming team-mates. The attacking midfielder (21), the forward (10) and the other winger (7) all make runs into the penalty area.

7. In this example, the ball is cut back to the attacking midfielder (21) to score in a central position.

Source: Pep Guardiola's Manchester City training session at Etihad Campus Training Ground, Manchester - 12th July 2017

4. Attacking Midfielder Moves Inside to Receive Forward's Lay-off, Dribble in Behind and Finish

Created using SoccerTutor.com Tactics Manager

Description

1. The right centre back (5) passes to the inverted right back (3).

2. The right back (3) passes inside to the defensive midfielder (25).

3. The defensive midfielder (25) passes to the forward (10), who drops back slightly.

4. The attacking midfielder (21) shifts across to receive the forward's lay-off.

5. The attacking midfielder (21) dribbles forward into the penalty area (and in behind).

6. The attacking midfielder (21) tries to score.

Source: Pep Guardiola's Manchester City training session at Etihad Campus Training Ground, Manchester - 12th July 2017

5. Attacking Midfielder's Pass in Behind to Winger from the "Half Space" After the Forward's Lay-off

Created using SoccerTutor.com Tactics Manager

Description

1. The right centre back (5) passes to the inverted right back (3).

2. The right back (3) passes inside to the defensive midfielder (25).

3. The defensive midfielder (25) passes to the forward (10), who drops back slightly.

4. The forward (10) passes to the attacking midfielder (17) in the "Half Space."

5. The attacking midfielder (17) plays a pass in behind for the run of the left winger (19).

6. The winger (19) moves forward with the ball.

7. The winger (19) cuts the ball back for oncoming team-mates. The attacking midfielder (21), the forward (10) and the other winger (7) all make runs into the penalty area.

8. In this example, the ball is cut back to the forward (10) to score in a central position.

Source: Pep Guardiola's Manchester City training session at Etihad Campus Training Ground, Manchester - 12th July 2017

35

6. Defensive Midfielder's Pass to the Forward + Lay-off to the Attacking Midfielder for Pass in Behind

Created using SoccerTutor.com Tactics Manager

Description

1. The right centre back (5) passes to the inverted right back (3).

2. The right back (3) passes inside to the defensive midfielder (25).

3. The defensive midfielder (25) passes to the forward (10), who drops back slightly.

4. The attacking midfielder (21) shifts inside to receive the forward's lay-off.

5. The attacking midfielder (21) plays a through pass in between the 2 central mannequins for the diagonal run of the other attacking midfielder (17).

6. The second attacking midfielder (17) receives and takes a touch out of his feet.

7. The attacking midfielder (17) tries to score.

Source: Pep Guardiola's Manchester City training session at Etihad Campus Training Ground, Manchester - 12th July 2017

7. Full Back's Pass to Forward + Lay-off to the Attacking Midfielder for a Pass in Behind

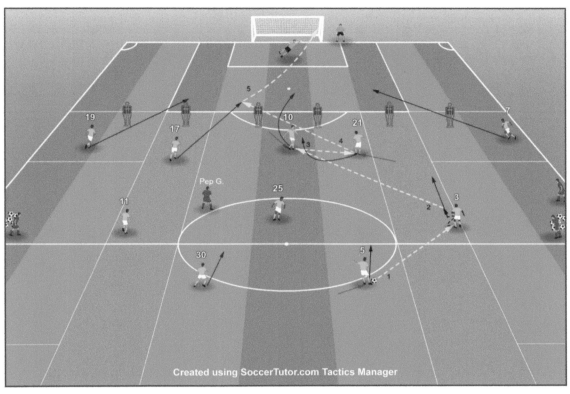

Created using SoccerTutor.com Tactics Manager

Description

1. The right centre back (5) passes to the inverted right back (3).

2. The right back (3) takes a touch forward and plays a diagonal pass to the forward (10), who drops back.

3. The forward (10) passes to the attacking midfielder (21), who moves inside to receive.

4. The attacking midfielder (21) plays a through pass in between the 2 central mannequins for the diagonal run of the other attacking midfielder (17).

5. The attacking midfielder (17) receives inside the penalty area and tries to score.

Source: Pep Guardiola's Manchester City training session at Etihad Campus Training Ground, Manchester - 12th July 2017

8. Defensive Midfielder's Diagonal Aerial Pass in Behind to the Winger + Cut Back

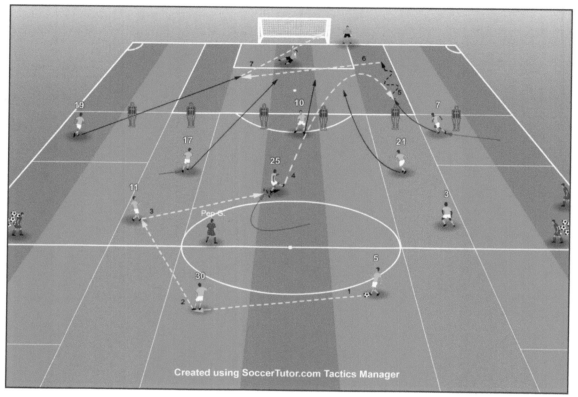

Created using SoccerTutor.com Tactics Manager

Description

1. The right centre back (5) passes to the left centre back (30).

2. The left centre back (30) passes to the inverted left back (11).

3. The left back (11) passes inside to the defensive midfielder (25), who has moved forward with a curved run.

4. The defensive midfielder (25) receives, opens up and plays a diagonal aerial pass in behind to the right winger (7).

5. The winger (7) receives and moves forward with the ball.

6. The winger (7) cuts the ball back for oncoming team-mates. The attacking midfielder (17), the forward (10) and the winger (19) all make runs into the penalty area

7. In this example, the ball is cut back to the winger (19) on the opposite side to score at the back post.

Source: Pep Guardiola's Manchester City training session at Etihad Campus Training Ground, Manchester - 12th July 2017

Attacking Positional Pattern of Play
Practice Variation: Add 1 Defender and
2 Midfield Mannequins

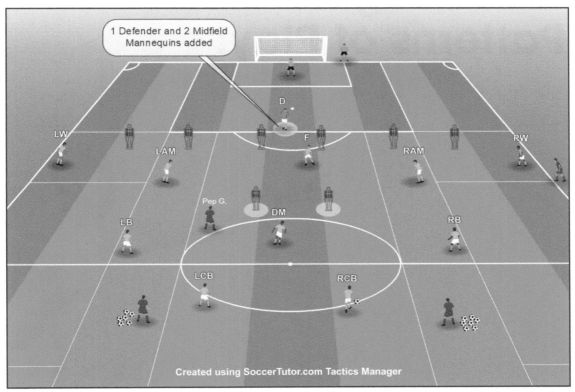

1 Defender and 2 Midfield Mannequins added

Created using SoccerTutor.com Tactics Manager

- This shows a variation of Pep Guardiola's positional attacking patterns of play displayed on the previous pages. The finishing of the attacks is now resisted by 1 defender and 2 midfield mannequins.

- The players practice the same patterns, but they now face 1 defender when trying to finish their attack in the penalty area.

- This can either be in a 1v1 situation after receiving a pass in behind the defensive line or the defender defends a low cross into the centre.

- In this variation, there are also 2 midfield mannequins added to create a more realistic situation with obstacles blocking forward passing lanes.

Source: Pep Guardiola's Manchester City training session at Etihad Campus Training Ground, Manchester - 8th May 2018

Attacking Positional Patterns of Play: 4-3-3 with Regular Full Backs

Direct from
Pep Guardiola's
Manchester City
Training Session

"He is a genius who reads the game and covers every situation imaginable. He is always showing us how to create space and find solutions and there is no manager like him, which makes him probably the best in the world."

(Ilkay Gündoğan)

PEP GUARDIOLA'S TRAINING SET-UP (REGULAR FULL BACKS)

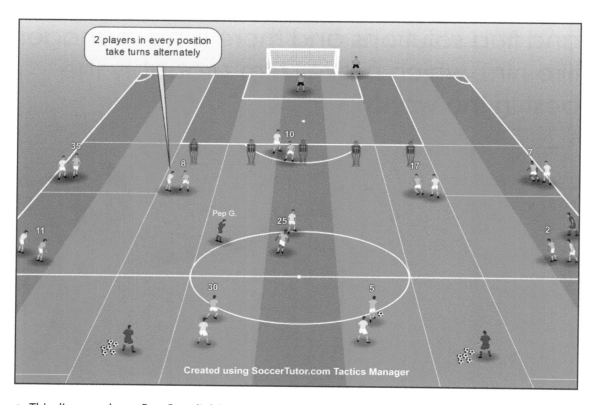

2 players in every position take turns alternately

Created using SoccerTutor.com Tactics Manager

- This diagram shows Pep Guardiola's set-up for practicing attacking positional patterns of play in the 4-3-3 with regular full backs.

- There are 5 mannequins and they are narrower than the previous patterns in the book.

- In each position, there are 2 players (1 blue and 1 yellow), which forms 2 teams of 10 outfield players to practice patterns. The 2 teams run the patterns outlined by Pep Guardiola alternately.

- The players have also changed from the previous patterns:

- **30. Otamendi:** Left Centre Back
- **5. Stones:** Right Centre Back
- **11. Kolarov:** Left Back
- **2. Walker:** Right Back
- **25. Fernandinho:** Defensive Midfielder
- **8. Gündoğan:** Left Attacking Midfielder
- **17. De Bruyne:** Right Attacking Midfielder
- **35. Zinchenko:** Left Winger
- **7. Sterling:** Right Winger
- **10. Agüero:** Forward

Source: Pep Guardiola's Manchester City preseason training session at NRG Stadium, Houston, Texas, USA - 20th July 2017

1. Forward's Lay-off from Defensive Midfielder's Pass for Attacking Midfielder to Play in Behind to Winger

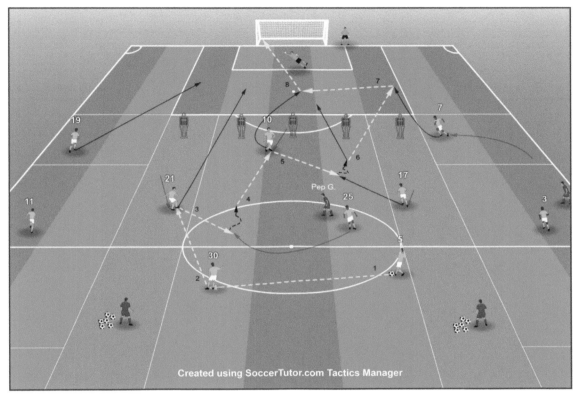

Created using SoccerTutor.com Tactics Manager

Description

1. The right centre back (5) passes to the left centre back (30).

2. The left centre back (30) passes to the attacking midfielder (21) in the "Half Space."

3. The defensive midfielder (25) shifts across (curved run) to receive the lay-off.

4. The defensive midfielder (25) moves forward with the ball and passes to the forward (10).

5. The forward (10) lays the ball back to the other attacking midfielder (17), who moves forward and inside to receive in the centre.

6. The second attacking midfielder (17) receives, opens up and plays a diagonal pass in behind to the winger (7).

7. The winger (7) receives and delivers a low cross for oncoming team-mates.

8. The attacking midfielder (21), both wingers (19 and 7) and the forward (10) all make runs into the penalty area to try and score. The forward (10) scores in this example.

Source: Pep Guardiola's Manchester City preseason training session at NRG Stadium, Houston, Texas, USA - 20th July 2017

43

2. Forward's "Dummy" of Defensive Midfielder's Pass for the Attacking Midfielder to Run onto and Score

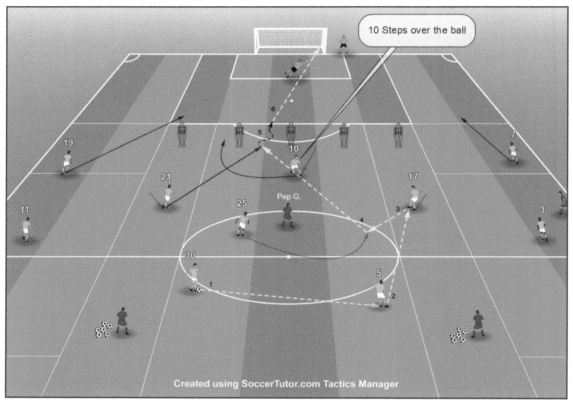

Description

1. The left centre back (30) passes across to the right centre back (5).

2. The right centre back (5) passes to the attacking midfielder (17) in the "Half Space."

3. The defensive midfielder (25) shifts across (curved run) to receive the lay-off.

4. The defensive midfielder (25) passes to the forward (10). However, the forward steps over the ball ("dummy").

5. The other attacking midfielder (21) on the left side makes a third man run to receive the ball after the "dummy" and move forward.

6. The attacking midfielder (21) shoots at goal.

Source: Pep Guardiola's Manchester City preseason training session at NRG Stadium, Houston, Texas, USA - 20th July 2017

3. Forward Plays Through Ball from Defensive Midfielder's Pass for the Attacking Midfielder's Third Man Run

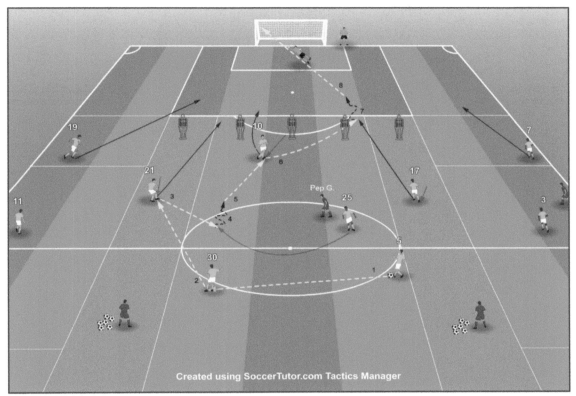

Created using SoccerTutor.com Tactics Manager

Description

1. The right centre back (5) passes across to the left centre back (30).

2. The left centre back (30) passes to the attacking midfielder (21) in the "Half Space."

3. The defensive midfielder (25) shifts across (curved run) to receive the lay-off.

4. The defensive midfielder (25) moves forward with the ball.

5. The defensive midfielder (25) passes to the forward (10).

6. The forward (10) drops back and plays first time in behind for the third man run of the other attacking midfielder (17).

7. The attacking midfielder (17) dribbles into the penalty area.

8. The attacking midfielder (17) finishes.

Source: Pep Guardiola's Manchester City preseason training session at NRG Stadium, Houston, Texas, USA - 20th July 2017

4. Defensive Midfielder's Combination Play in the Centre + Diagonal Aerial Pass in Behind to the Winger

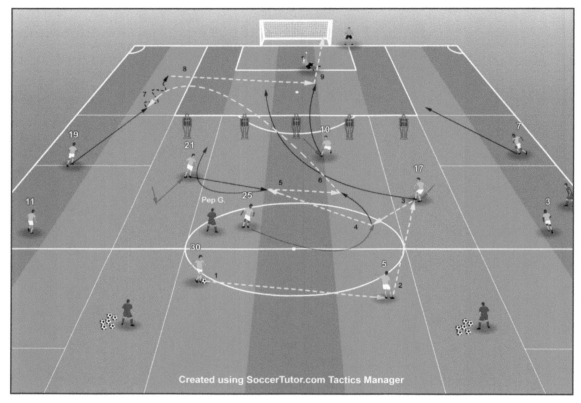

Created using SoccerTutor.com Tactics Manager

Description

1. The left centre back (30) passes across to the right centre back (5).

2. The right centre back (5) passes to the attacking midfielder (17) in the "Half Space."

3. The defensive midfielder (25) shifts across (curved run) to receive the lay-off.

4. The defensive midfielder (25) passes to the attacking midfielder (21) on the left side, who moves into a central position to receive.

5. The defensive midfielder (25) moves forward to receive the lay-off.

6. The defensive midfielder (25) plays a diagonal aerial pass in behind to the left winger (19).

7. The winger (19) dribbles forward with the ball.

8. The winger (19) delivers a low cross for oncoming team-mates.

9. The forward (10) scores from a central position.

Source: Pep Guardiola's Manchester City preseason training session at NRG Stadium, Houston, Texas, USA - 20th July 2017

Attacking Positional Patterns of Play (4-3-3)

Direct from
Pep Guardiola's
FC Barcelona
Training Sessions

"I had a unique master. I grew a lot with Pep as a player and learnt a great deal from him. Some managers are superb tacticians, but Pep would also describe the moves you had to make on the pitch and what would happen then. And it did!"

(Lionel Messi)

PEP GUARDIOLA'S FC BARCELONA FORMATION (4-3-3)

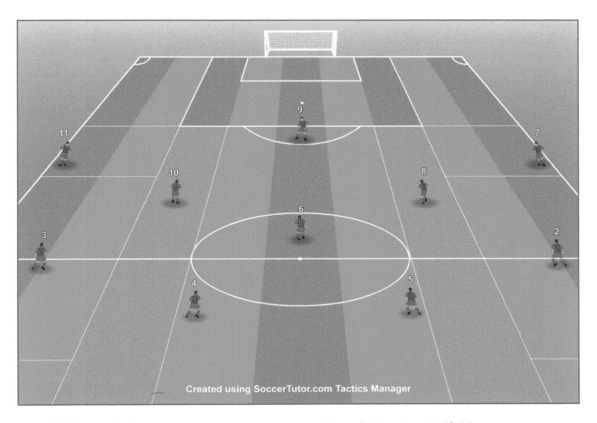

Created using SoccerTutor.com Tactics Manager

- **4:** Left Centre Back
- **5:** Right Centre Back
- **3:** Left Back
- **2:** Right Back
- **6:** Defensive Midfielder

- **10:** Left Attacking Midfielder
- **8:** Right Attacking Midfielder
- **11:** Left Winger
- **7:** Right Winger
- **9:** Forward

Source: Pep Guardiola's training sessions from Barcelona B team (2007-08)

POSITIONING AND RECEIVING IN THE "HALF SPACES" (4-3-3)

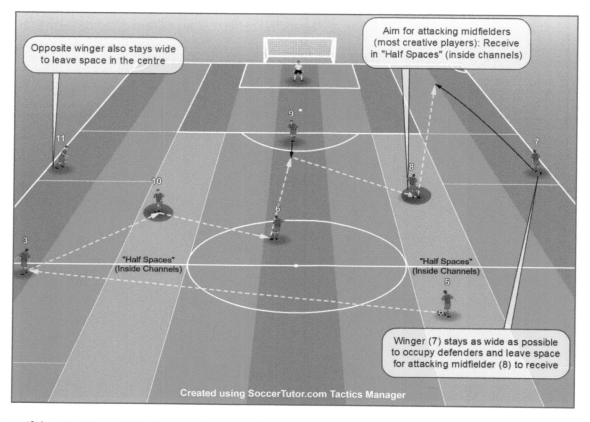

Opposite winger also stays wide to leave space in the centre

Aim for attacking midfielders (most creative players): Receive in "Half Spaces" (inside channels)

"Half Spaces" (Inside Channels)

"Half Spaces" (Inside Channels)

Winger (7) stays as wide as possible to occupy defenders and leave space for attacking midfielder (8) to receive

Created using SoccerTutor.com Tactics Manager

- If the attacking midfielders receive unmarked within the "Half Spaces" and are able to turn, they then try to play a final pass in behind.

- Pep Guardiola wants his wingers (**7 & 11**) to stay wide to occupy the defenders and leave space for his attacking midfielders to receive within the "Half Space" and turn unmarked.

- In this example, FC Barcelona are using the 4-3-3 and the defensive midfielder (**6**) passes to the forward (**9**), who drops back and passes to the attacking midfielder (**8**) within the "Half Space."

- The attacking midfielder (**8**) has options to play a pass in behind.

- In the diagram example, the attacking midfielder (**8**) plays in behind for the forward run of the right winger (**7**).

- From this point, the right winger (**7**) will deliver a low cross or a cut back for oncoming team-mates who make well-timed runs into the penalty area.

Source: Pep Guardiola's training sessions from Barcelona B team (2007-08)

1. Switching Play for the Winger to Receive High Up and in Behind Using Short/Medium Passes

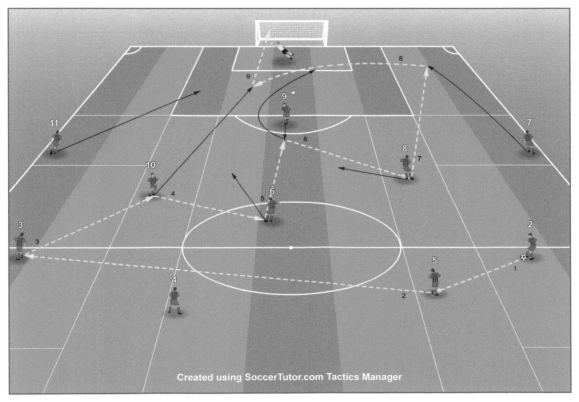

Created using SoccerTutor.com Tactics Manager

Description

1. The right back (2) passes inside to the centre back (5).

2. The centre back (5) passes across to the left back (3), evading the other centre back (4).

3. The left back (3) passes to the attacking midfielder (10), who receives within the "Half Space."

4. The attacking midfielder (10) passes inside to the defensive midfielder (6) in the centre.

5. The defensive midfielder (6) passes forward to the forward (9), who drops back.

6. The forward (9) lays the ball back to the other attacking midfielder (8), who also receives within the "Half Space."

7. Pep Guardiola wants his best and most creative players to receive within the "Half Space" - from here, No.8 can play a pass in behind for the right winger (7).

8. The winger (7) crosses for oncoming team-mates to score.

Source: Pep Guardiola's training sessions from Barcelona B team (2007-08)

2. Switching Play with a Long Pass for the Winger to Receive and Dribble Forward

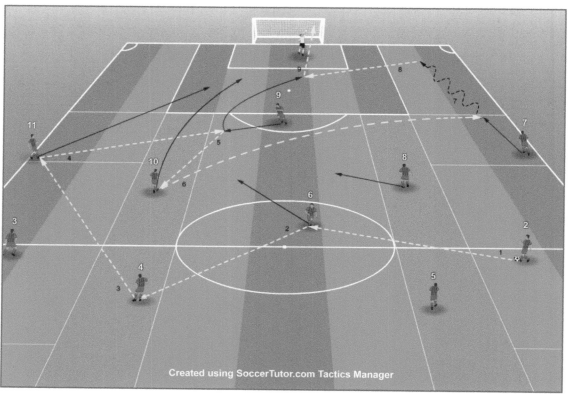

Created using SoccerTutor.com Tactics Manager

Description

1. The right back (2) passes inside to the defensive midfielder (6) in the centre.

2. The defensive midfielder (6) passes back to the left centre back (4).

3. The left centre back (4) plays a medium length pass out wide to the winger (11).

4. The winger (11) passes inside to the forward (9), who moves across to receive.

5. The forward (9) passes back for the attacking midfielder (10) to receive in the "Half Space."

6. After combination play on one side, the aim is now to move the ball quickly to the weak side and exploit the space out wide. The attacking midfielder (10) plays a long pass to switch play to the opposite winger (7).

7. The winger (7) dribbles forward.

8. The winger (7) crosses for oncoming team-mates to score.

Source: Pep Guardiola's training sessions from Barcelona B team (2007-08)

3. Attacking Through the Centre with an Aerial Pass in Behind and the Attacking Midfielder's Third Man Run

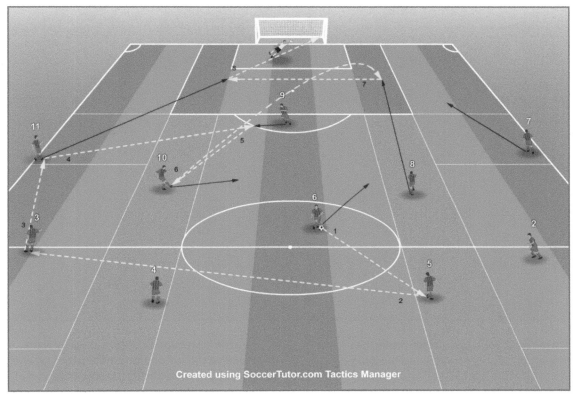

Created using SoccerTutor.com Tactics Manager

Description

1. The defensive midfielder (6) passes back to the right centre back (5).

2. The right centre back (5) passes across to the left back (3), evading the other centre back (4).

3. The left back (3) passes forward to the winger (11) out wide.

4. The winger (11) passes inside to the forward (9), who moves across to receive.

5. The forward (9) plays the ball back to the attacking midfielder (10), who receives within the "Half Space."

6. The other attacking midfielder (8) makes a third man run and No.10 plays a well-timed diagonal aerial pass into his path and in behind.

7. The attacking midfielder (8) crosses (cut back) for the winger (11) to score.

Source: Pep Guardiola's training sessions from Barcelona B team (2007-08)

4. Timing of Movement to Combine, Receive On the Overlap, Cross and Finish

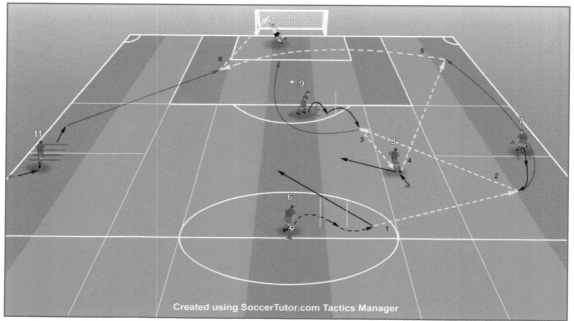

Created using SoccerTutor.com Tactics Manager

Objective: High ball speed, timing of movement, concentration and finishing.

Description

1. The defensive midfielder (6) dribbles through the poles, passes out wide to the winger (7) and runs forward into the centre.

2. The right winger (7) jumps over the hurdle, moves back to receive the defensive midfielder's (6) pass and plays a diagonal pass to the forward (9). He then makes a run up the line.

3. The forward (9) jumps over the hurdle, runs around the pole to receive the winger's (7) pass and passes back to the attacking midfielder (8). He then makes a curved run into the penalty area.

4. The attacking midfielder (8) moves forward to receive the lay-off from the forward (9) and plays a pass out wide for the advanced run of the winger (7). He then moves inside.

5. The right winger (7) receives the pass in an advanced position after an overlapping run and crosses into the penalty area.

6. The left winger (11) skips through the ground poles and makes a run to the far post to try and score from the cross.

All players rotate positions. Allow sufficient recovery time so each pattern of play is performed at a high speed. This pattern can also be performed on the opposite side.

Source: Pep Guardiola's training sessions from Barcelona B team (2007-08)

5. Timing of Movement to Combine, Switch Play, Cross and Finish

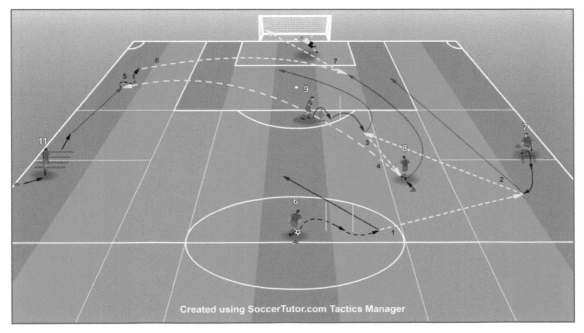

Created using SoccerTutor.com Tactics Manager

Objective: High ball speed, timing of movement, concentration and finishing.

Description

1. The defensive midfielder (6) dribbles through the poles, passes out wide to the winger (7) and runs forward into the centre.

2. The right winger (7) jumps over the hurdle, moves back to receive the defensive midfielder's (6) pass and plays a diagonal pass to the forward (9). He then makes a run towards the back post.

3. The forward (9) jumps over the hurdle, runs around the pole to receive the winger's (7) pass and passes back to the attacking midfielder (8). He then makes a curved run towards the front post.

4. The attacking midfielder (8) moves forward to receive the lay-off from the forward (9) and switches play with a diagonal aerial pass to the left winger (11). He then makes a curved run in between the other 2 players.

5. The left winger (11) skips through the ground poles, makes a forward run to receive the switch of play and delivers a cross into the penalty area.

All players rotate positions. Allow sufficient recovery time so each pattern of play is performed at a high speed. This pattern can also be performed on the opposite side.

Source: Pep Guardiola's training sessions from Barcelona B team (2007-08)

6. Four Player Attacking Combination with Through Pass, Cross and Finish On the Left Side

This is a more focused pattern of play with the full back in possession in the opposition's half. The pattern includes 4 players: Left back (3), attacking midfielder (10), winger (11) and forward (9).

Description

1. The left winger (11) has his back to goal and passes back to the left back (3).

2. The left back (3) passes diagonally to the forward (9).

3. The forward (9) passes back to the attacking midfielder (10) and then starts his movement towards the penalty area.

4. The attacking midfielder (10) plays a longer pass into an advanced position high up the flank for the left winger (11) to run onto.

5. The left winger (11) crosses into the centre of the penalty area for the well-timed run of the forward (9), who tries to score.

Source: Pep Guardiola's training sessions from Barcelona B team (2007-08)

7. Four Player Attacking Combination with Through Pass, Cross and Finish On the Right Side

Created using SoccerTutor.com Tactics Manager

This is a more focused pattern of play with the full back in possession in the opposition's half. The pattern includes 4 players: Right back (2), attacking midfielder (8), winger (7) and forward (9).

Description

1. The right back (2) passes forward to the right winger (7).

2. The right winger (7) passes back to the right back (2) to complete a 1-2 combination, and then turns to run forward.

3. The right back (2) passes to the forward (9).

4. The forward (9) passes back to the attacking midfielder (8) and then starts his movement towards the penalty area.

5. The attacking midfielder (8) plays a longer pass into an advanced position high up the flank for the right winger (7) to run onto.

6. The right winger (7) crosses into the centre of the penalty area for the well-timed run of the forward (9), who tries to score.

Source: Pep Guardiola's training sessions from Barcelona B team (2007-08)

ATTACKING POSITIONAL PATTERNS OF PLAY (3-5-2)

"While we attack, the idea is to always keep your position, always being in the place you have to be. The is dynamism, mobility, but the position has always got to be filled by someone."

PEP GUARDIOLA'S MANCHESTER CITY FORMATION (3-5-2)

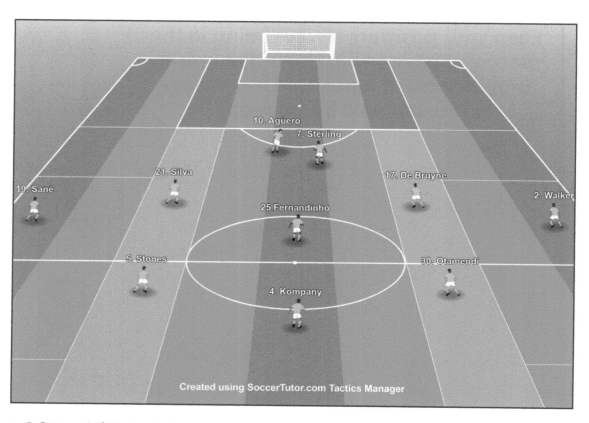

Created using SoccerTutor.com Tactics Manager

- **5. Stones:** Left Centre Back

- **4. Kompany:** Middle Centre Back

- **30. Otamendi:** Right Centre Back

- **19. Sané:** Left Wing Back

- **2. Walker:** Right Wing Back

- **25. Fernandinho:** Defensive Midfielder

- **21. Silva:** Left Attacking Midfielder

- **17. De Bruyne:** Right Attacking Midfielder

- **7. Sterling:** Second Forward

- **10. Agüero:** Centre Forward

Source: Pep Guardiola's Manchester City training session during preseason tour of USA - Nissan Stadium, Nashville 29th July 2017

POSITIONING AND RECEIVING IN THE "HALF SPACES" (3-5-2)

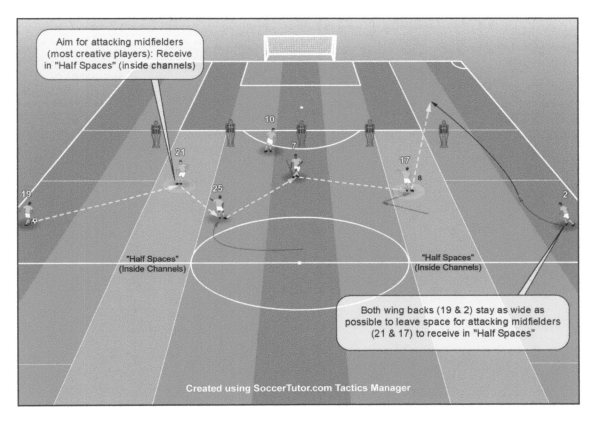

Aim for attacking midfielders (most creative players): Receive in "Half Spaces" (inside channels)

"Half Spaces" (Inside Channels)

"Half Spaces" (Inside Channels)

Both wing backs (19 & 2) stay as wide as possible to leave space for attacking midfielders (21 & 17) to receive in "Half Spaces"

Created using SoccerTutor.com Tactics Manager

- If the Manchester City attacking midfielders receive unmarked within the "Half Spaces" and are able to turn, they then try to play a final ball in behind.

- Pep Guardiola wants his wing backs **(19 & 2)** to stay wide and leave space for his attacking midfielders to receive within the "Half Space" and turn unmarked.

- In this example, Manchester City are using the 3-5-2 formation and the second forward **Sterling (7)** passes to the attacking midfielder **De Bruyne (17)** within the "Half Space."

- From this point, **De Bruyne (17)** has options to play a pass in behind.

- In the diagram example, **De Bruyne (17)** passes in behind for the right wing back **Walker (2)** to run onto.

Source: Pep Guardiola's Manchester City training session during preseason tour at Nissan Stadium, Nashville, USA - 29th July 2017

PEP GUARDIOLA'S TRAINING SET-UP FOR PATTERNS (3-5-2)

2 players in every position take turns alternately

Pep G.

Created using SoccerTutor.com Tactics Manager

- This diagram shows Pep Guardiola's set-up for practicing positional patterns of play in training with his Manchester City team.

- There are coaches behind with many balls, ready to pass to the centre backs to start the pattern.

- There are also 5 mannequins in a line outside the penalty area and 3 passive red defenders in the centre.

- In each position, there are 2 players (1 blue and 1 yellow), which forms 2 teams of 10 outfield players to practice patterns.

- The 2 teams run the patterns outlined by Pep Guardiola alternately.

- As soon as one team finishes, they jog back to their positions and the next team goes.

Source: Pep Guardiola's Manchester City training session during preseason tour at Nissan Stadium, Nashville, USA - 29th July 2017

Defensive Midfielder's Pass for Forward's Lay-off with Third Man Runs Through the Centre

Direct from
Pep Guardiola's
Manchester City
Training Session

1. Both Forwards Drop Back to Combine + Attacking Midfielder's Third Man Run in Behind

Created using SoccerTutor.com Tactics Manager

Description

1. The left centre back (5) passes inside to the middle centre back (4).

2. The middle centre back (4) passes across to the right centre back (30).

3. The right centre back (30) passes to the attacking midfielder (17), who drops back and receives within the "Half Space."

4. The defensive midfielder (25) moves across to receive the lay-off pass.

5. The defensive midfielder (25) passes to the advanced forward (10), who drops back to receive.

6. The forward (10) lays the ball back to the other forward (7), who is in a deeper position

7. The attacking midfielder (17) makes a third man run and receives the forward's (7) well-timed pass in behind.

8. The attacking midfielder (17) passes across to the forward (10), who has made a curved run to get into position to score.

Source: Pep Guardiola's Manchester City training session during preseason tour at Nissan Stadium, Nashville, USA - 29th July 2017

2. Forward's Lay-off to 2nd Forward + Attacking Midfielder's Third Man Run to Receive in Centre

Created using SoccerTutor.com Tactics Manager

Description

1. The right centre back (30) passes inside to the middle centre back (4).

2. The middle centre back (4) passes across to the left centre back (5).

3. The left centre back (5) passes to the attacking midfielder (21) within the "Half Space."

4. The defensive midfielder (25) moves across and forward to receive the lay-off pass.

5. The defensive midfielder (25) passes to the forward (10), and the other forward (7) drops.

6. The forward (10) lays the ball back to the other forward (7).

7. The attacking midfielder on the other side (17) makes a well-timed third man run to receive the forward's (7) pass.

8. The attacking midfielder (17) dribbles forward between the mannequins and shoots at goal.

Source: Pep Guardiola's Manchester City training session during preseason tour at Nissan Stadium, Nashville, USA - 29th July 2017

3. Forward's Lay-off to 2nd Forward + Attacking Midfielder's Third Man Run in Behind

Created using SoccerTutor.com Tactics Manager

Description

1. The right centre back (30) passes inside to the middle centre back (4).

2. The middle centre back (4) passes to the attacking midfielder (21) on the left side, who drops back and receives within the "Half Space."

3. The defensive midfielder (25) initially drops back to receive from No.4, and then moves across to receive the inside pass from the attacking midfielder (21).

4. The defensive midfielder (25) moves forward with the ball and passes to the forward (10).

5. The forward (10) lays the ball back to the other forward (7).

6. The attacking midfielder (21) makes a third man run and receives the forward's (7) well-timed pass in behind.

7. The attacking midfielder (17) passes across to the forward (10) who has made a forward run to get into position to score.

Source: Pep Guardiola's Manchester City training session during preseason tour at Nissan Stadium, Nashville, USA - 29th July 2017

4. Fast Combination Play Between the Attacking Midfielder and 2 Forwards

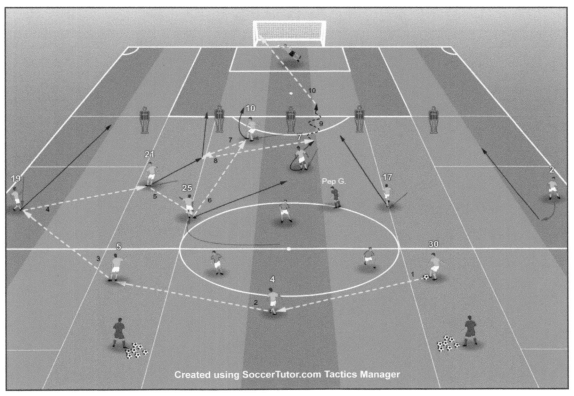

Created using SoccerTutor.com Tactics Manager

Description

1. The right centre back (30) passes inside to the middle centre back (4).

2. The middle centre back (4) passes across to the left centre back (5).

3. The left centre back (5) passes to the left wing back (19), who receives out wide.

4. The left wing back (19) passes to the attacking midfielder (21) within the "Half Space."

5. The defensive midfielder (25) moves across and forward to receive the lay-off pass.

6. The defensive midfielder (25) passes to the forward (10), and the other forward (7) drops back.

7. The forward (10) lays the ball back to the attacking midfielder (21), who again receives within the "Half Space."

8. The attacking midfielder (21) plays a well-timed pass into the centre for the movement of the forward (7).

9. The forward (7) dribbles forward between the mannequins and shoots at goal.

Source: Pep Guardiola's Manchester City training session during preseason tour at Nissan Stadium, Nashville, USA - 29th July 2017

67

5. Using the Defensive Midfielder's Fast Combinations to Build Up Play to the Forwards

Created using SoccerTutor.com Tactics Manager

Description

1. The right centre back (30) passes inside to the middle centre back (4).

2. The middle centre back (4) dribbles across.

3. The middle centre back (4) passes to the defensive midfielder (25).

4. The defensive midfielder (25) plays the ball back to complete the 1-2 combination.

5. The middle centre back (4) passes across to the left centre back (5).

6. The left centre back (5) passes to the attacking midfielder (21), who receives within the "Half Space."

7. The defensive midfielder (25) moves forward (curved run) to receive the lay-off.

8. The defensive midfielder (25) passes to the forward (10).

9. The forward (10) passes across for the other forward (7) to run onto, dribble forward and shoot at goal.

Source: Pep Guardiola's Manchester City training session during preseason tour at Nissan Stadium, Nashville, USA - 29th July 2017

Switching the Point of Attack and Passing in Behind to the Wing Back

Direct from
Pep Guardiola's
Manchester City
Training Session

1. Switching Play for the Wing Back to Receive in Behind with Overlap Run

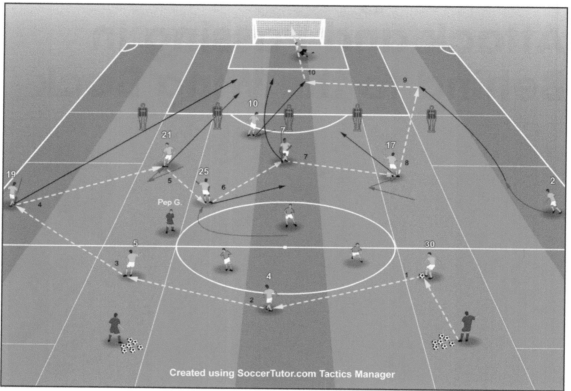

Created using SoccerTutor.com Tactics Manager

Description

1. The right centre back (30) passes inside to the middle centre back (4).

2. The middle centre back (4) passes across to the left centre back (5).

3. The left centre back (5) passes to the left wing back (19), who receives out wide.

4. The left wing back (19) passes to the attacking midfielder (21) within the "Half Space."

5. The defensive midfielder (25) moves across and forward to receive the lay-off pass.

6. The defensive midfielder (25) passes to the forward (7), who drops back to receive.

7. The forward (7) lays the ball back to the other attacking midfielder (17), who also receives within the "Half Space."

8. The attacking midfielder (17) passes in behind for the right wing back's (2) overlapping run.

9. The wing back (2) crosses for oncoming team-mates to score.

Source: Pep Guardiola's Manchester City training session during preseason tour at Nissan Stadium, Nashville, USA - 29th July 2017

2. Defensive Midfielder's Aerial Switch of Play to the Wing Back + Attacking Midfielder's Third Man Run

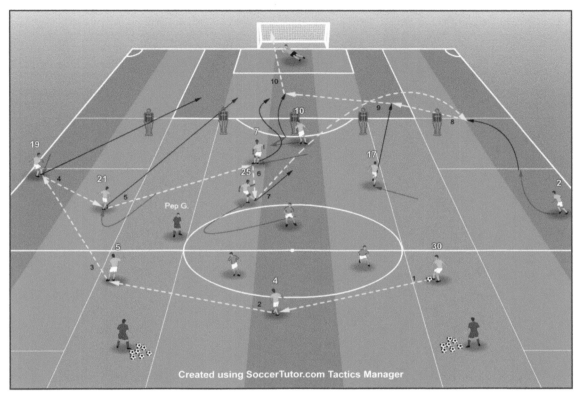

Created using SoccerTutor.com Tactics Manager

Description

1. The right centre back (30) passes inside to the middle centre back (4).

2. The middle centre back (4) passes across to the left centre back (5).

3. The left centre back (5) passes to the left wing back (19), who receives out wide.

4. The left wing back (19) passes back to the attacking midfielder (21), who moves across.

5. The attacking midfielder (21) passes to the forward (7), who moves across to receive.

6. The forward (7) lays the ball back to the defensive midfielder (25), who has made a curved run.

7. The right wing back (2) makes a forward run to receive the defensive midfielder's (25) aerial pass. The other attacking midfielder (17) makes a third man run in between the mannequins.

8. The wing back (2) passes inside to the attacking midfielder (17).

9. The attacking midfielder (17) passes across for the forward (10) to score.

Source: Pep Guardiola's Manchester City training session during preseason tour at Nissan Stadium, Nashville, USA - 29th July 2017

3. Using Short Combination Play to Switch the Point of Attack in Behind to the Wing Back

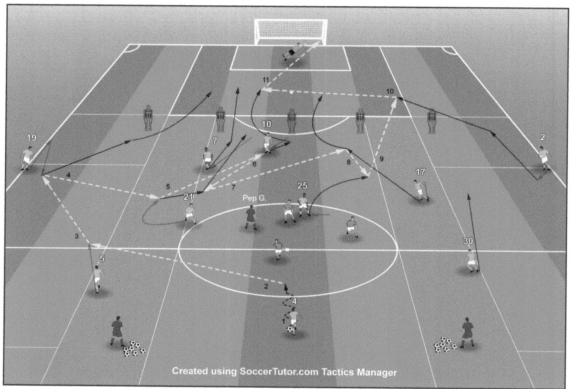

Created using SoccerTutor.com Tactics Manager

Description

1. The middle centre back (4) dribbles forward.

2. The middle centre back (4) passes to the left centre back (5), who moves forward.

3. The left centre back (5) passes to the left wing back (19), who drops back.

4. The attacking midfielder (25) moves across to receive the next pass within the "Half Space."

5. The attacking midfielder (25) passes to the forward (10), who drops back.

6. The forward (10) plays the ball back to the attacking midfielder (21) to complete the 1-2 combination.

7. The attacking midfielder (21) passes to the other attacking midfielder (17), who has moved into an advanced position.

8. The defensive midfielder (25) moves forward to receive the lay-off.

9. The defensive midfielder (25) plays the ball in behind for the wing back (2) to run onto and deliver a low cross for oncoming team-mates.

Source: Pep Guardiola's Manchester City training session during preseason tour at Nissan Stadium, Nashville, USA - 29th July 2017

4. Forward's Lay-off to 2nd Forward to Switch the Point of Attack in Behind to the Wing Back

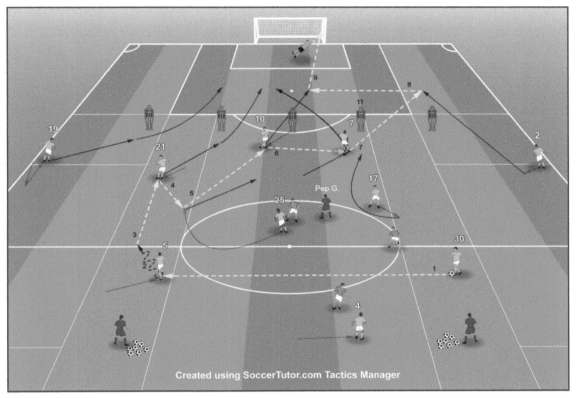

Created using SoccerTutor.com Tactics Manager

* A red opponent is in a more advanced position to block the pass to the middle centre back (4).

Description

1. The right centre back (30) passes across to the left centre back (5).

2. The left centre back (5) dribbles forward.

3. The left centre back (5) passes to the attacking midfielder (21) within the "Half Space."

4. The defensive midfielder (25) drops back and then moves forward (curved run) to receive the lay-off from the attacking midfielder (21).

5. The defensive midfielder (25) passes to the forward (10).

6. The forward (10) passes across to the second forward (7).

7. The second forward (7) passes in behind to the right wing back (2), who makes a forward run.

8. The right wing back (2) delivers a low cross for the forward (10) to score.

Source: Pep Guardiola's Manchester City training session during preseason tour at Nissan Stadium, Nashville, USA - 29th July 2017

5. Combination Play with Defensive Midfielder + Pass in Behind to the Wing Back on the Weak Side

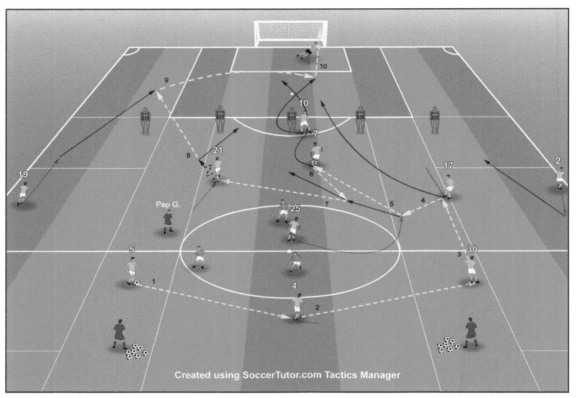

Created using SoccerTutor.com Tactics Manager

Description

1. The left centre back (5) passes inside to the middle centre back (4).

2. The middle centre back (4) passes across to the right centre back (30).

3. The right centre back (30) passes to the attacking midfielder (17), who drops back and receives within the "Half Space."

4. The defensive midfielder (25) moves across and forward to receive the lay-off pass.

5. The defensive midfielder (25) passes to the forward (7), who drops back to receive.

6. The forward (7) lays the ball back to the defensive midfielder (25) to complete the 1-2 combination.

7. The defensive midfielder (25) passes across to the other attacking midfielder (21), who dribbles forward.

8. The attacking midfielder (21) passes in behind for the left wing back's (19) diagonal run.

9. The left wing back (19) delivers a cross for the forward (10) to score.

Source: Pep Guardiola's Manchester City training session during preseason tour at Nissan Stadium, Nashville, USA - 29th July 2017

6. Forward's Lay-off to Switch Attack to the Weak Side Attacking Midfielder + Pass in Behind to Wing Back

Created using SoccerTutor.com Tactics Manager

Description

1. The left centre back (5) passes inside to the middle centre back (4).

2. The middle centre back (4) passes across to the right centre back (30).

3. The right centre back (30) passes to the right wing back (2), who receives out wide.

4. The wing back (2) passes to the attacking midfielder (17) within the "Half Space."

5. The defensive midfielder (25) moves across to receive the lay-off pass.

6. The defensive midfielder (25) passes to the second forward (7), who drops back to receive.

7. The second forward (7) passes across to the other attacking midfielder (21).

8. The attacking midfielder (21) passes in behind for the left winger's (19) diagonal run.

9. The winger (19) delivers a low cross for oncoming team-mates.

Source: Pep Guardiola's Manchester City training session during preseason tour at Nissan Stadium, Nashville, USA - 29th July 2017

Forward's Lay-off for Attacking Midfielder to Pass in Behind

Direct from
Pep Guardiola's
Manchester City
Training Session

"It's impossible against a deep defence to be narrow. First be wide and then after that, runs in behind."

Source: Pep Guardiola Interview with Transversales on SFR Sport 1, France - February 2018

1. Attacking Midfielder's Aerial Pass from the Centre to the Advanced Wing Back

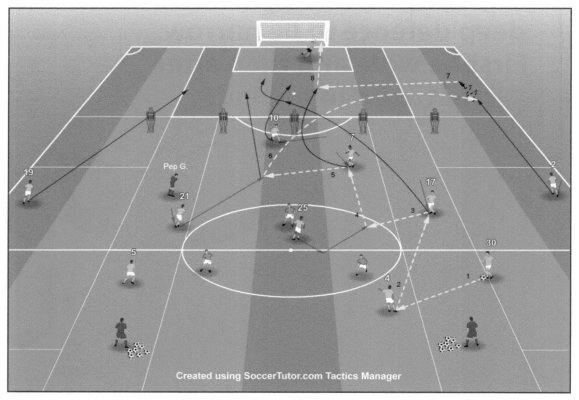

Created using SoccerTutor.com Tactics Manager

Description

1. The right centre back (30) passes inside to the middle centre back (4).

2. The middle centre back (4) passes to the attacking midfielder (17), who drops back and receives within the "Half Space."

3. The defensive midfielder (25) drops back and then moves across to receive the lay-off pass.

4. The defensive midfielder (25) passes to the second forward (7), who moves back to receive.

5. The second forward (7) passes across for the other attacking midfielder (21) to run onto.

6. The attacking midfielder (21) plays an aerial pass in behind for the wing back's (2) forward run.

7. The wing back (2) delivers a low cross for oncoming team-mates.

Source: Pep Guardiola's Manchester City training session during preseason tour at Nissan Stadium, Nashville, USA - 29th July 2017

2. Attacking Midfielder Receiving Advanced Forward's Lay-off On the Run + Pass in Behind to the Wing Back

Created using SoccerTutor.com Tactics Manager

Description

1. The right centre back (30) passes inside to the middle centre back (4).

2. The middle centre back (4) passes to the attacking midfielder (17), who drops back and receives within the "Half Space."

3. The defensive midfielder (25) moves across to receive the lay-off pass.

4. The defensive midfielder (25) moves forward with the ball and passes to the forward (10), who moves across to receive.

5. The forward (10) lays the ball back for the other attacking midfielder (21) to run onto.

6. The attacking midfielder (21) passes in behind for the wing back's (19) forward run.

7. The wing back (19) cuts the ball back for the attacking midfielder (21).

8. The attacking midfielder (21) shoots and tries to score.

Source: Pep Guardiola's Manchester City training session during preseason tour at Nissan Stadium, Nashville, USA - 29th July 2017

79

3. Attacking Midfielder Receiving Deep Forward's Lay-off On the Run + Pass in Behind to Wing Back (1)

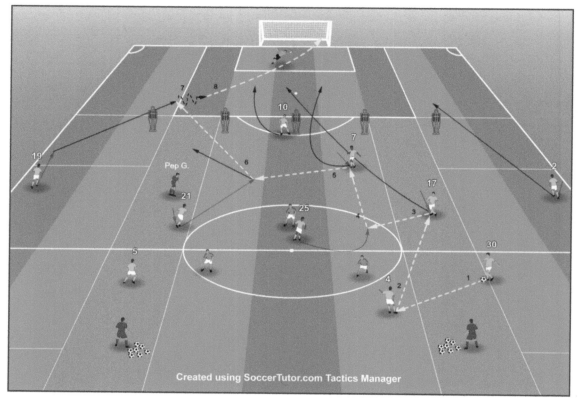

Created using SoccerTutor.com Tactics Manager

Description

1. The right centre back (30) passes inside to the middle centre back (4).

2. The middle centre back (4) passes to the attacking midfielder (17), who drops back and receives within the "Half Space."

3. The defensive midfielder (25) moves across to receive the lay-off pass.

4. The defensive midfielder (25) passes to the deep forward (7), who moves back to receive.

5. The forward (7) passes across for the other attacking midfielder (21) to run onto.

6. The attacking midfielder (21) passes in behind for the wing back's (19) run.

7. The wing back (19) cuts inside and shoots.

Source: Pep Guardiola's Manchester City training session during preseason tour at Nissan Stadium, Nashville, USA - 29th July 2017

4. Attacking Midfielder Receiving Deep Forward's Lay-off On the Run + Pass in Behind to Wing Back (2)

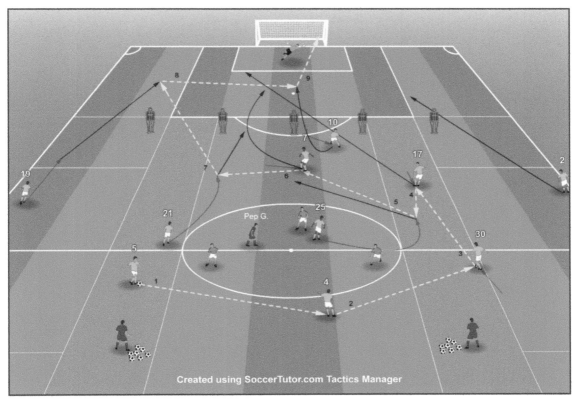

Created using SoccerTutor.com Tactics Manager

Description

1. The left centre back (5) passes inside to the middle centre back (4).

2. The middle centre back (4) passes across to the right centre back (30).

3. The right centre back (30) passes to the attacking midfielder (17), who drops back and receives within the "Half Space."

4. The defensive midfielder (25) moves across and forward (curved run) to receive the lay-off pass.

5. The defensive midfielder (25) passes to the deep forward (7), who moves across to receive.

6. The forward (7) passes across for the other attacking midfielder (21) to run onto.

7. The attacking midfielder (21) receives the forward's (7) pass and plays in behind for the left wing back's (19) diagonal run.

8. The left wing back (19) delivers a low cross for oncoming team-mates.

Source: Pep Guardiola's Manchester City training session during preseason tour at Nissan Stadium, Nashville, USA - 29th July 2017

5. Passing Through the Lines + Wing Back's Third Man Run to Receive in Behind

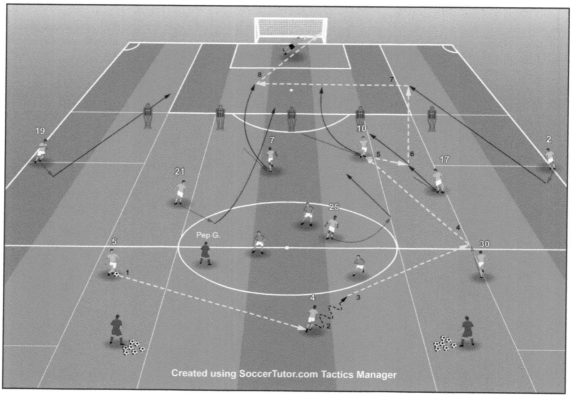

Created using SoccerTutor.com Tactics Manager

Description

1. The left centre back (5) passes back to the middle centre back (4).

2. The middle centre back (4) dribbles across to the right slightly and is closed down.

3. The middle centre back (4) passes to the right centre back (30), who moves forward.

4. The right centre back (30) passes to the forward (10), who drops and shifts across to the right.

5. The attacking midfielder (17) moves to receive the lay-off pass within the "Half Space."

6. The attacking midfielder (17) passes in behind to the right wing back (2), who makes a diagonal forward run.

7. The right wing back (2) delivers a low cross for oncoming team-mates.

Source: Pep Guardiola's Manchester City training session during preseason tour at Nissan Stadium, Nashville, USA - 29th July 2017

6. Attacking Midfielder Receiving Advanced Forward's Lay-off + Pass in Behind to the 2nd Forward

Created using SoccerTutor.com Tactics Manager

Description

1. The middle centre back (4) dribbles forward with the ball and there is pressure from a red opponent.

2. The middle centre back (4) passes to the left centre back (5), who has moved forward.

3. The left centre back (5) passes to the attacking midfielder (21), who receives within the "Half Space."

4. The defensive midfielder (25) moves forward (curved run) to receive the lay-off.

5. The defensive midfielder (25) passes to the forward (10), who moves across to the left side.

6. The forward (10) lays the ball off for the attacking midfielder (21) to run onto and receive within the "Half Space."

7. The attacking midfielder (21) plays a through ball in between the mannequins for the second forward (7) to receive in behind and score.

Source: Pep Guardiola's Manchester City training session during preseason tour at Nissan Stadium, Nashville, USA - 29th July 2017

PEP GUARDIOLA STOPS THE TRAINING SESSION AT THIS POINT AND MAKES THE FOLLOWING CHANGES:

- The Left Attacking Midfielder (21) drops back next to the Defensive Midfielder (25)

- The Defensive Midfielder (25) shifts to the right slightly

- In many of the patterns to follow, the 2nd Forward (7) drops back and moves into the "Half Space" to receive

- 1 red opponent is removed

Attacking Midfielder Drops Back and the Forward Moves into "Half Space" to Link Play

Direct from
Pep Guardiola's
Manchester City
Training Session

1. Forward Receives Lay-off in "Half Space" and Passes Inside for Attacking Midfielder to Dribble in Behind

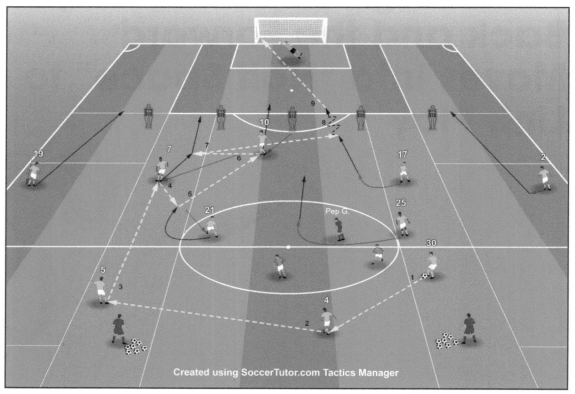

Created using SoccerTutor.com Tactics Manager

Description

1. The right centre back (30) passes back to the middle centre back (4).

2. The middle centre back (4) passes across to the left centre back (5).

3. The attacking midfielder (21) drops back. The left centre back (5) passes to the forward (7), who has shifted across to receive within the "Half Space."

4. The attacking midfielder (21) now moves forward to receive the forward's (7) lay-off.

5. The attacking midfielder (21) passes to the advanced forward (10), who drops back.

6. The forward (10) passes across for the second forward (7) to run onto.

7. The forward (10) passes across for the attacking midfielder on the other side (17) to run onto.

8. The attacking midfielder (17) dribbles in between the mannequins, into the penalty area and shoots at goal.

Source: Pep Guardiola's Manchester City training session during preseason tour at Nissan Stadium, Nashville, USA - 29th July 2017

2. Double Lay-off for Defensive Midfielder's Pass in Behind to the Wing Back

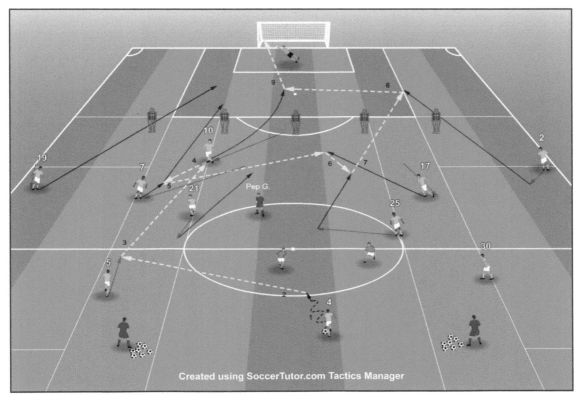

Created using SoccerTutor.com Tactics Manager

Description

1. The middle centre back (4) dribbles forward with the ball and there is pressure from a red opponent.

2. The middle centre back (4) passes to the left centre back (5), who has moved forward.

3. The left centre back (5) passes to the forward (10), who shifts across to receive.

4. The second forward (7) had previously shifted across to the left side, and now makes a forward movement to receive the lay-off.

5. The second forward (7) passes to the attacking midfielder (17), who moves into the centre to receive.

6. The defensive midfielder (25) moves forward to receive the lay-off.

7. The defensive midfielder (25) passes in behind for the right wing back's (2) run.

8. Both forwards (7 & 10) and the left wing back (19) make runs into the penalty area. The right wing back (2) delivers a low cross for the forward (10) to score.

Source: Pep Guardiola's Manchester City training session during preseason tour at Nissan Stadium, Nashville, USA - 29th July 2017

3. Wing Back's One-Two with the Forward in the "Half Space" to Receive in Behind

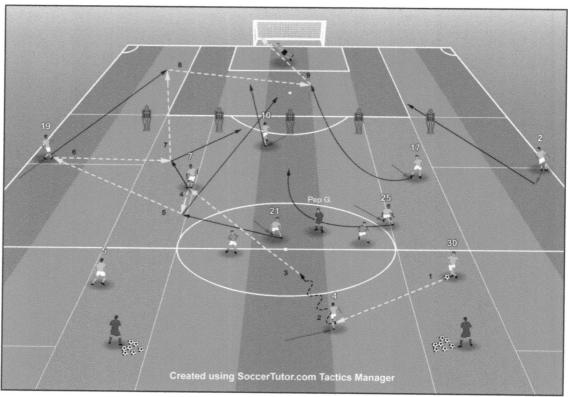

Created using SoccerTutor.com Tactics Manager

* The attacking midfielder (21) is in a central position and the forward (7) is in a wide position.

Description

1. The right centre back (30) passes inside to the middle centre back (4).

2. The middle centre back (4) dribbles forward with the ball.

3. The middle centre back (4) passes to the forward (7) within the "Half Space."

4. The attacking midfielder (21) moves across to receive the lay-off.

5. The attacking midfielder (21) passes to the left wing back (19).

6. The left wing back (19) passes inside to the forward (7) within the "Half Space."

7. The forward (7) plays the ball in behind for the wing back (19) to run onto and completes the 1-2 combination.

8. The wing back (19) delivers a low cross for oncoming team-mates.

Source: Pep Guardiola's Manchester City training session during preseason tour at Nissan Stadium, Nashville, USA - 29th July 2017

4. Wing Back Checks Back and Makes a Forward Run to Receive Out Wide and in Behind from the Forward

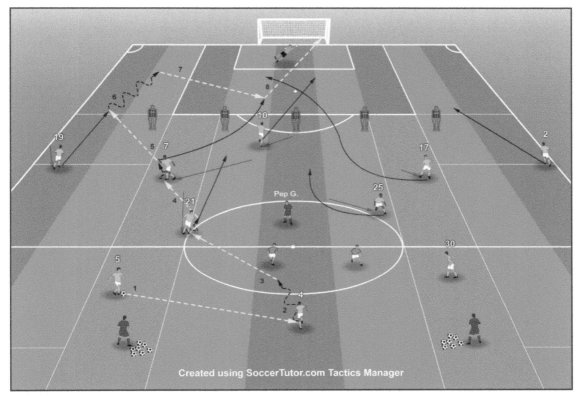

Created using SoccerTutor.com Tactics Manager

Description

1. The left centre back (5) passes inside to the middle centre back (4).

2. The middle centre back (4) dribbles forward with the ball and there is pressure from an opponent.

3. The middle centre back (4) passes to the attacking midfielder (17), who drops back.

4. The attacking midfielder (17) turns and passes to the forward (7), who has shifted across to receive within the "Half Space."

5. The forward (7) turns and passes out wide and in behind to the left wing back (19).

6. The left wing back (19) receives and dribbles the ball forward.

7. The left wing back (19) cuts the ball back for the forward (7) to score.

Source: Pep Guardiola's Manchester City training session during preseason tour at Nissan Stadium, Nashville, USA - 29th July 2017

5. Attacking Midfielder Drops Back and the Forward Shifts Across to Combine Within "Half Space" and Switch Play

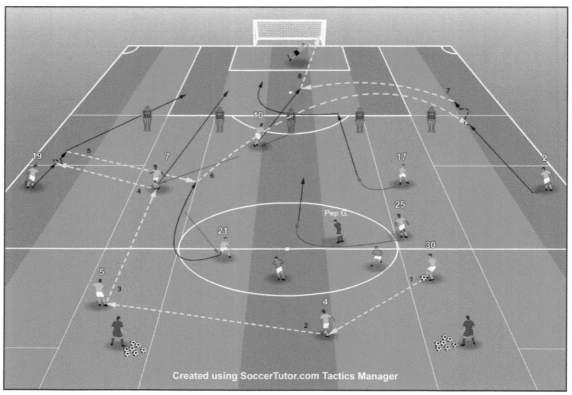

Created using SoccerTutor.com Tactics Manager

Description

1. The right centre back (30) passes back to the middle centre back (4).

2. The middle centre back (4) passes across to the left centre back (5).

3. The attacking midfielder (21) drops back. The left centre back (5) passes to the forward (7), who has shifted across to receive within the "Half Space."

4. The forward (7) passes out wide to the left wing back (19).

5. The attacking midfielder (21) now moves forward to receive the wing back's (19) inside pass.

6. The attacking midfielder (21) plays a long aerial pass for the forward run of the right wing back (2).

7. The right wing back (2) receives, dribbles forward and crosses for oncoming team-mates.

Source: Pep Guardiola's Manchester City training session during preseason tour at Nissan Stadium, Nashville, USA - 29th July 2017

6. Switching Play from One Wing Back to the Other with the Attacking Midfielder's Aerial Pass

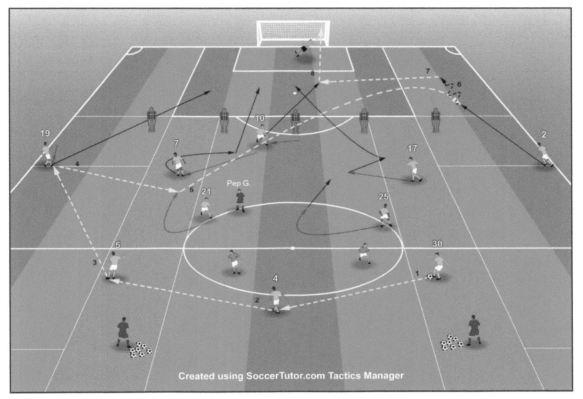

Created using SoccerTutor.com Tactics Manager

Description

1. The right centre back (30) passes inside to the middle centre back (4).

2. The middle centre back (4) passes across to the left centre back (5).

3. The left centre back (5) passes to the left wing back (19), who receives out wide.

4. The left wing back (19) passes inside to the attacking midfielder (21), who moves forward from his deep position to receive within the "Half Space."

5. The attacking midfielder (21) plays a long aerial pass in behind to the advanced right wing back (2).

6. The right wing back (2) receives in behind the defensive line, dribbles forward and crosses for oncoming team-mates.

Source: Pep Guardiola's Manchester City training session during preseason tour at Nissan Stadium, Nashville, USA - 29th July 2017

7. Forward Shifts Across into the "Half Space" to Lay-off for Attacking Midfielder's Pass to the Wing Back

Created using SoccerTutor.com Tactics Manager

Description

1. The left centre back (5) passes inside to the middle centre back (4).

2. The middle centre back (4) passes to the attacking midfielder (17) in the "Half Space."

3. The attacking midfielder (17) lays the ball off to the right centre back (5), who moves forward.

4. The right centre back (5) passes to the second forward (7), who has shifted across to receive within the "Half Space."

5. The attacking midfielder (17) moves forward to receive the lay-off pass.

6. The attacking midfielder (17) passes in behind for the right wing back's (2) forward run.

7. Both forwards (7 & 10), the attacking midfielder (21) and the left wing back (19) make runs into the penalty area. The right wing back (2) crosses for his oncoming team-mates.

Source: Pep Guardiola's Manchester City training session during preseason tour at Nissan Stadium, Nashville, USA - 29th July 2017

8. Advanced Forward's Lay-off for 2nd Forward to Play a Diagonal Aerial Pass in Behind to the Wing Back

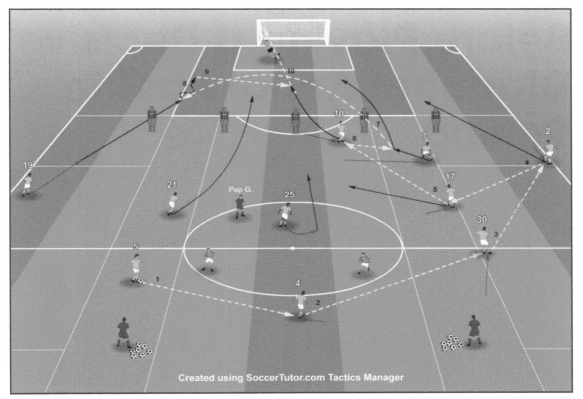

Created using SoccerTutor.com Tactics Manager

Description

1. The left centre back (5) passes inside to the middle centre back (4).

2. The middle centre back (4) passes across to the right centre back (30), who moves forward.

3. The right centre back (30) passes out wide to the advanced right wing back (2).

4. The right wing back (2) passes inside to the attacking midfielder (17), who receives within the "Half Space." The forward (7) shifts across.

5. The attacking midfielder (17) passes to the forward (10).

6. The forward (10) lays the ball back to the second forward (7) inside the "Half Space."

7. The second forward (7) plays a diagonal aerial pass to the left wing back (19) on the weak side.

8. The left wing back (19) receives and moves forward with the ball.

9. The left wing back (19) cuts the ball back for the forward (10) to score.

Source: Pep Guardiola's Manchester City training session during preseason tour at Nissan Stadium, Nashville, USA - 29th July 2017

Consolidating Possession Before Playing a Decisive Diagonal Aerial Pass in Behind

Direct from
Pep Guardiola's
Manchester City
Training Session

1. Fast Combination Play in the Centre and Short Diagonal Aerial Pass in Behind to the Forward

Created using SoccerTutor.com Tactics Manager

Description

1. The left centre back (5) passes inside to the middle centre back (4).

2. The middle centre back (4) passes across to the right centre back (30).

3. The right centre back (30) passes to the forward (7), who shifts across to receive within the "Half Space."

4. The attacking midfielder (17) moves forward to receive the lay-off pass.

5 & 6. The attacking midfielder (17) plays a 1-2 with the defensive midfielder (25).

7. The attacking midfielder (17) passes inside to the other attacking midfielder (21), who has moved inside and forward to receive.

8. The attacking midfielder (17) lays the ball back to the defensive midfielder (25).

9. The defensive midfielder (25) passes to the left wing back (19) out wide.

10. The left wing back (19) passes inside to the attacking midfielder (21).

11 & 12. The attacking midfielder (21) receives and plays an aerial pass in behind to the forward (7), who cuts the ball back for No.10.

Source: Pep Guardiola's Manchester City training session during preseason tour at Nissan Stadium, Nashville, USA - 29th July 2017

2. Combination Play with Multiple Lay-offs + Diagonal Aerial Pass in Behind to the Forward

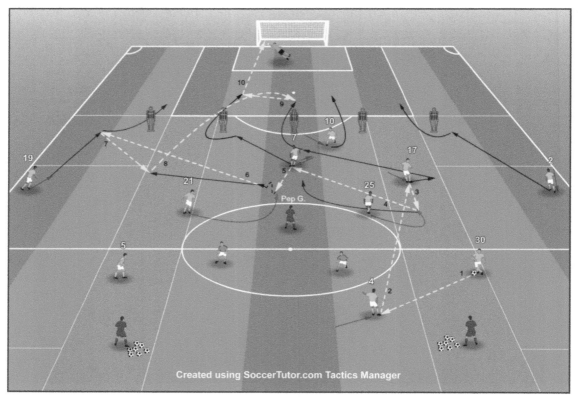

Created using SoccerTutor.com Tactics Manager

Description

1. The right centre back (30) passes back to the middle centre back (4).

2. The middle centre back (4) passes to the attacking midfielder (17) within the "Half Space."

3. The defensive midfielder (25) moves to receive the attacking midfielder's (17) lay-off.

4. The defensive midfielder (25) passes to the forward (7).

5. The forward (7) passes back for the other attacking midfielder (21) to run onto.

6. The attacking midfielder (21) passes out wide to the left wing back (19).

7. The left wing back (19) passes back to the attacking midfielder (21), who shifts across to receive within the "Half Space."

8. The attacking midfielder (21) plays an aerial pass in behind to the forward (10).

9. The forward (10) passes the ball for the second forward (7) to score.

Source: Pep Guardiola's Manchester City training session during preseason tour at Nissan Stadium, Nashville, USA - 29th July 2017

3. Fast Combination Play in the Centre with Lay-offs + Diagonal Aerial Pass in Behind to the Wing Back (1)

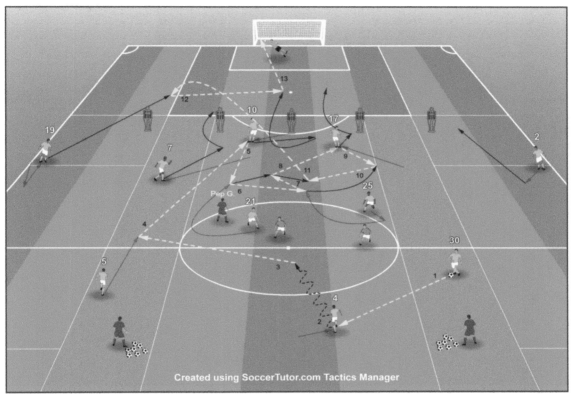

Created using SoccerTutor.com Tactics Manager

Description

1. The right centre back (30) passes inside to the middle centre back (4).

2. The middle centre back (4) dribbles forward with the ball.

3. The middle centre back (4) passes across to the left centre back (5), who moves forward.

4. The left centre back (5) passes to the forward (10).

5. The attacking midfielder (21) moves forward (curved run) to receive back from No.10.

6 & 7. The attacking midfielder (21) plays a 1-2 with the defensive midfielder (25).

8. The attacking midfielder (21) passes to the other attacking midfielder (17), who has moved into an advanced position.

9. The defensive midfielder (25) moves across to receive back from No.17.

10. The defensive midfielder (25) passes inside to the attacking midfielder (21).

11. The attacking midfielder (21) plays an aerial pass in behind to the wing back (19).

Source: Pep Guardiola's Manchester City training session during preseason tour at Nissan Stadium, Nashville, USA - 29th July 2017

4. Switching Play from One Wing Back to the Other and Back Again with a Lay-off + Diagonal Aerial Pass in Behind

Created using SoccerTutor.com Tactics Manager

Description

1. The left centre back (5) passes inside to the middle centre back (4).

2. The middle centre back (4) dribbles forward.

3. The middle centre back (4) passes to the left centre back (5).

4. The left centre back (5) passes out wide to the left wing back (19).

5. The left wing back (19) passes inside to the attacking midfielder (21) in the "Half Space."

6. The attacking midfielder (21) passes to the forward (7), who moves into the "Half Space."

7. The forward (7) passes to the defensive midfielder (25) in the centre.

8. The defensive midfielder (25) passes to the right centre back (30), who moves forward.

9. The right centre back (30) passes to the right wing back (2), who has moved forward.

10. The right wing back (2) passes back to the attacking midfielder (17), who shifts across.

11. The attacking midfielder (17) plays an aerial pass in behind to the left wing back (19).

Source: Pep Guardiola's Manchester City training session during preseason tour at Nissan Stadium, Nashville, USA - 29th July 2017

5. Fast Combination Play in the Centre with Lay-offs + Diagonal Aerial Pass in Behind to the Wing Back (2)

Created using SoccerTutor.com Tactics Manager

Description

1. The right centre back (30) passes back to the middle centre back (4).

2. The middle centre back (4) dribbles forward.

3. The middle centre back (4) passes to the left centre back (5) within the "Half Space."

4. The left centre back (5) passes to the forward (7), who has shifted across to receive within the "Half Space."

5. The attacking midfielder (21) moves forward (curved run) to receive the lay-off.

6. The attacking midfielder (21) passes to the forward (10).

7. The attacking midfielder (17) on the right side moves across to receive the lay-off.

8. The attacking midfielder (17) passes out wide to the left wing back (19).

9. The forward (7) moves across to receive the lay-off.

10. The forward (7) plays an aerial pass in behind to the wing back (2) on the other side, who cuts the ball back to No.10.

Source: Pep Guardiola's Manchester City training session during preseason tour at Nissan Stadium, Nashville, USA - 29th July 2017

6. Fast Combination Play Within the "Half Space" + Diagonal Aerial Pass in Behind to the Opposite Wing Back

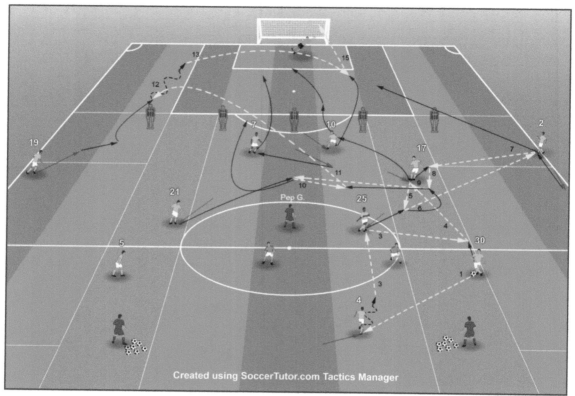

Created using SoccerTutor.com Tactics Manager

Description

1. The right centre back (5) passes back to the middle centre back (4).

2. The middle centre back (4) moves forward and passes to the defensive midfielder (25).

3. The defensive midfielder (25) passes to the right centre back (30).

4. The right centre back (30) passes to the attacking midfielder (17).

5. The defensive midfielder (25) moves to receive the lay-off pass.

6. The defensive midfielder (25) passes out wide to the right wing back (2).

7. The right wing back (2) passes to the attacking midfielder (17) in the "Half Space."

8. The defensive midfielder (25) moves to receive the lay-off pass.

9 & 10. The defensive midfielder (25) plays a 1-2 with the attacking midfielder (21) on the other side, who moves into the centre.

11. The defensive midfielder (25) plays an aerial pass in behind to the left wing back (19).

Source: Pep Guardiola's Manchester City training session during preseason tour at Nissan Stadium, Nashville, USA - 29th July 2017

Combination Play with the Wing Back Using Give-and-Go and Underlap Runs

Direct from
Pep Guardiola's
Manchester City
Training Session

1. Double One-Two Combination for the Wing Back to Receive in Behind (1)

Created using SoccerTutor.com Tactics Manager

Description

1. The right centre back (30) passes inside to the middle centre back (4).

2. The middle centre back (4) passes to the defensive midfielder (25) in the centre.

3. The defensive midfielder (25) passes to the attacking midfielder in the "Half Space."

4. The attacking midfielder (21) plays the ball back to complete the 1-2 combination.

5. The defensive midfielder (25) passes to the left wing back (19), who receives high up.

6. The left wing back (19) passes inside for the forward run of the attacking midfielder (21).

7. The attacking midfielder (21) plays the ball in behind for the wing back (19) to run onto and completes the second 1-2 combination.

8. The wing back (19) delivers a low cross for oncoming team-mates.

Source: Pep Guardiola's Manchester City training session during preseason tour at Nissan Stadium, Nashville, USA - 29th July 2017

2. Double One-Two Combination for the Wing Back to Receive in Behind (2)

Created using SoccerTutor.com Tactics Manager

Description

1. The left centre back (5) passes back to the middle centre back (4).

2. The middle centre back (4) dribbles forward.

3. The middle centre back (4) passes to the defensive midfielder (25).

4. The defensive midfielder (25) passes to the attacking midfielder (17) in the "Half Space."

5. The defensive midfielder (25) receives the attacking midfielder's (17) lay-off pass in the "Half Space" to complete the 1-2 combination.

6. The defensive midfielder (25) passes out wide to the right wing back (2), who initially checks back and then moves forward to receive.

7. The right wing back (2) passes inside to the attacking midfielder (17) in the "Half Space."

8. The attacking midfielder (17) passes in behind for the right wing back (2) to run onto and completes the 1-2 combination.

9. The right wing back (2) delivers a low cross for oncoming team-mates.

Source: Pep Guardiola's Manchester City training session during preseason tour at Nissan Stadium, Nashville, USA - 29th July 2017

3. Play Out Wide to the Wing Back + Pass in Behind for the Attacking Midfielder's Underlap Run

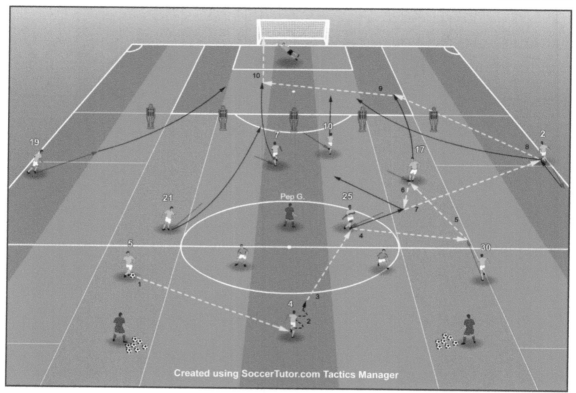

Created using SoccerTutor.com Tactics Manager

Description

1. The left centre back (5) passes back to the middle centre back (4).

2. The middle centre back (4) moves forward with the ball.

3. The middle centre back (4) passes to the defensive midfielder (25).

4. The defensive midfielder (25) passes to the right centre back (30).

5. The right centre back (30) passes to the attacking midfielder (17).

6. The defensive midfielder (25) moves to receive the lay-off pass.

7. The defensive midfielder (25) passes out wide to the advanced right wing back (2).

8. The right wing back (2) passes in behind to the attacking midfielder (17), who makes an underlapping run in behind.

9. The attacking midfielder (17) passes across for oncoming team-mates to score.

Source: Pep Guardiola's Manchester City training session during preseason tour at Nissan Stadium, Nashville, USA - 29th July 2017

(104)

4. Switching Play to the Wing Back + Pass in Behind for the Attacking Midfielder's Underlap Run

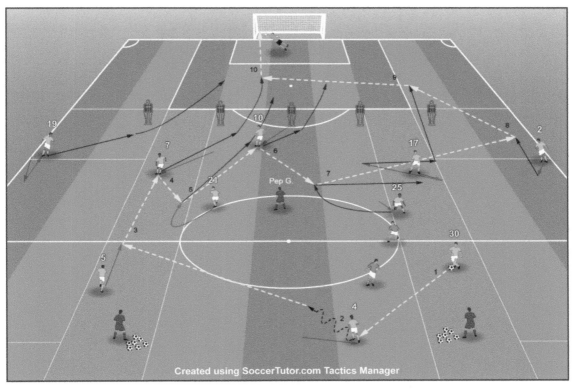

Created using SoccerTutor.com Tactics Manager

Description

1. The right centre back (30) passes back to the middle centre back (4).

2. The middle centre back (4) dribbles across to the left slightly.

3. The middle centre back (4) passes to the left centre back (5), who moves forward.

4. The left centre back (5) passes to the forward (7), who shifts across to receive within the "Half Space."

5. The attacking midfielder (17) moves to receive the lay-off pass in the "Half Space."

6. The attacking midfielder (17) passes to the advanced forward (10) in a central position.

7. The defensive midfielder (25) moves to receive the lay-off pass.

8. The defensive midfielder (25) passes out wide to the right wing back (2), who initially checks back and then moves forward to receive.

9. The right wing back (2) passes to the attacking midfielder (17), who makes an underlapping to receive in behind.

Source: Pep Guardiola's Manchester City training session during preseason tour at Nissan Stadium, Nashville, USA - 29th July 2017

5. Forward Passing Through Lines and One-Two Combination Out Wide with Attacking Midfielder's Underlap Run

Created using SoccerTutor.com Tactics Manager

Description

1. The left centre back (5) passes back to the middle centre back (4).

2. The middle centre back (4) dribbles forward.

3. The middle centre back (4) passes to the defensive midfielder (25), who checks away before moving to receive.

4. The defensive midfielder (25) passes to the attacking midfielder (21) in the "Half Space."

5. The attacking midfielder (21) passes for the left wing back (19) to run onto.

6. The left wing back (19) passes in behind to the attacking midfielder (21), who makes an underlapping run in behind.

7. The attacking midfielder (21) cuts the ball back for the forward (10) to score.

Source: Pep Guardiola's Manchester City training session during preseason tour at Nissan Stadium, Nashville, USA - 29th July 2017

Attacking Midfielder's Penetrating Run to Receive and Dribble Through Centre

Direct from
Pep Guardiola's
Manchester City
Training Session

1. Fast Combination Play in and Around the "Half Space" + Pass into Centre for Att. Midfielder to Dribble in Behind

Created using SoccerTutor.com Tactics Manager

Description

1. The left centre back (5) passes back to the middle centre back (4).

2. The middle centre back (4) moves forward with the ball.

3. The middle centre back (4) passes to the defensive midfielder (25).

4. The defensive midfielder (25) passes to the right centre back (30).

5. The right centre back (30) passes to the forward (10).

6. The attacking midfielder (17) moves to receive the lay-off pass within the "Half Space."

7. The right attacking midfielder (17) passes to the left attacking midfielder (21), who moves forward and into the centre.

8. The attacking midfielder (21) receives and dribbles between the mannequins and towards goal.

9. The attacking midfielder (21) shoots from outside the penalty area.

Source: Pep Guardiola's Manchester City training session during preseason tour at Nissan Stadium, Nashville, USA - 29th July 2017

2. Both Forwards Shift Across to Combine and Create Space for the Att. Midfielder to Dribble in Behind

Created using SoccerTutor.com Tactics Manager

Description

1. The right centre back (30) passes back to the middle centre back (4).

2. The middle centre back (4) dribbles across to the left slightly.

3. The middle centre back (4) passes to the left centre back (5), who moves forward.

4. The left centre back (5) passes to the forward (10), who shifts across slightly.

5. The second forward (7) has shifted across to the left within the "Half Space", then moves

forward to receive the lay-off pass.

6. The second forward (7) passes to the right attacking midfielder (17), who moves forward and towards the centre.

7. The attacking midfielder (17) receives and dribbles between the mannequins and towards goal.

8. The attacking midfielder (17) shoots from inside the penalty area.

Source: Pep Guardiola's Manchester City training session during preseason tour at Nissan Stadium, Nashville, USA - 29th July 2017

ATTACKING COMBINATIONS & FINISHING

"My football is simple: I like to attack, attack and attack."

"I love to attack. That's my idea of football. It is the speed of the attack that will intrigue."

Attacking Combination Play to Create Chances and Finish

Direct from
Pep Guardiola's
Manchester City
Training Sessions

1. Passing and Showing to Receive in an Attacking Combination with Lay-off, Dribble and Finish

Player D sprints around the 2 red cones to take up Position E

Description

1. Player A passes to B, who drops back behind the pole.

2. Player B passes back for A to move forward onto, completing the 1-2 combination.

3. Player B passes to C.

4. Player C passes across to B, who has moved forward past the pole.

5. Player B passes forward to D, who drops back.

6. Player D plays a lay-off pass for E to move forward onto.

7. Player E receives and dribbles past the mannequin.

8. Player E shoots at goal.

9. The players rotate positions:
   (A -> B -> C -> D -> E -> A).

Source: Pep Guardiola's Manchester City training session at Etihad Campus Training Ground, Manchester - 12th July 2017

2. Passing Combination, One-Two to Receive in Behind and Finish

> Player D sprints around the 2 red cones to take up Position E

Description

- In this variation of the previous practice, Player E does not dribble forward after receiving the lay-off from D.

- Instead, Player E plays a 1-2 combination with D and shoots after receiving the return pass in behind the mannequin.

- The players rotate positions: (A -> B -> C -> D -> E -> A).

Source: Pep Guardiola's Manchester City training session at Etihad Campus Training Ground, Manchester - 12th July 2017

3. Passing Combination + Receive Ground Pass On the Run, One-Two and Shoot

Created using SoccerTutor.com Tactics Manager

Description

1. Player A passes back to B.

2. Player B passes to A to complete the 1-2 combination.

3. Player A passes diagonally to D.

4. Player D passes across to B, who has dropped back to receive.

5. Player B passes back to C.

6. Player C plays the longest pass of the sequence for D to run onto (curved run through the red cones as shown).

7. Player D dribbles forward and is put under passive pressure by the Coach.

8. Player A passes to E.

9 & 10. Player E plays a return pass for A to run onto (1-2 combination) and shoot.

11. The players rotate positions:
(A -> B -> C -> D -> E -> A).

Source: Pep Guardiola's Manchester City training session at Etihad Campus Training Ground, Manchester - 3rd May 2018

4. Passing Combination + Receive Aerial Pass On the Run, One-Two and Shoot

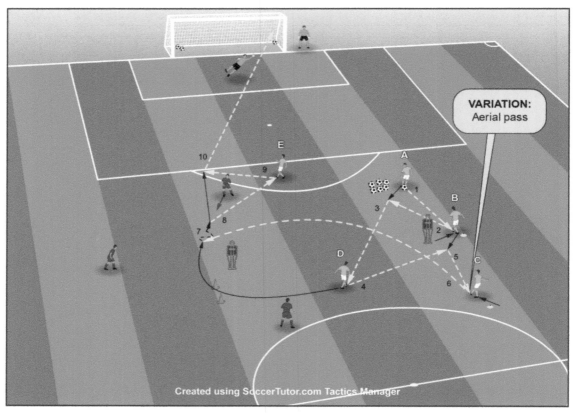

> **VARIATION:**
> Aerial pass

Description

- In this variation of the previous practice, Player C uses an aerial pass instead of a pass along the ground.

- The rest of the practice is the same as the previous.

- The players rotate positions:
  (A -> B -> C -> D -> E -> A).

Source: Pep Guardiola's Manchester City training session at Etihad Campus Training Ground, Manchester - 3rd May 2018

5. Passing Combination and Diagonal Aerial Pass in Behind for a Third Man Run + Finish

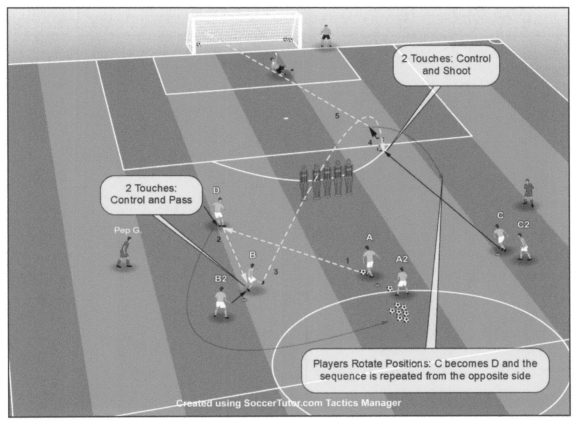

Description

1. Player A passes diagonally to D.

2. Player D drops back and passes to B.

3. Player C has timed a forward run. Player B controls the ball and plays an aerial pass over the mannequins (2 touches), timed well for C to run onto.

4 & 5. Player C controls and shoots (2 touches).

6. The players rotate positions.

7. The practice is repeated on the opposite side, with Player C taking the role of D.

Source: Pep Guardiola's Manchester City training session at Etihad Campus Training Ground, Manchester

6. One-Two, Pass Wide and in Behind, Cross and Finish

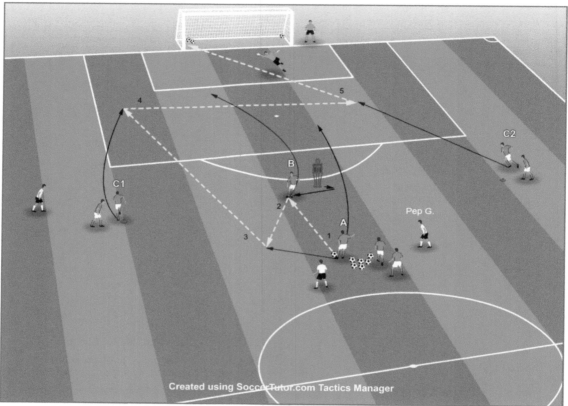

Created using SoccerTutor.com Tactics Manager

Description

1. Player A passes to B, who checks away from the mannequin before moving to receive.

2. Player A moves across to receive the pass back from B (completes the 1-2 combination).

3. Player A receives and passes in behind to C1's run into the penalty area.

4. Player C1 receives after a well-timed forward run and delivers a low cross for oncoming team-mates.

5. Players A, B and C2 have all made runs into the penalty area to try and score from the low cross. Player C2 scores in the diagram example.

6. Repeat the sequence on the opposite side: The next Player A plays a 1-2 with B and then passes in behind for C2 to cross.

Source: Pep Guardiola's Bayern Munich training session at Säbener Strasse Training Ground, Munich - 13th November 2014

7. One-Two, Diagonal Aerial Pass in Behind and Forward Run to Score from Cut Back

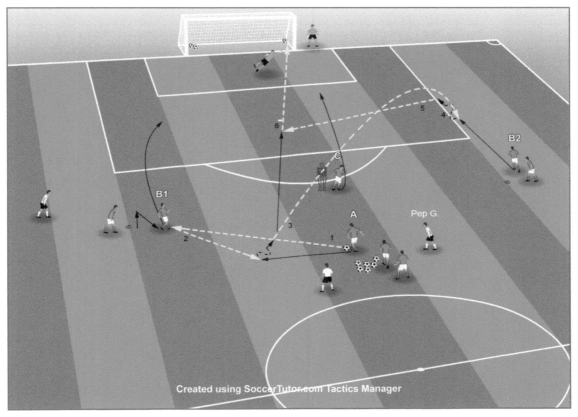

Created using SoccerTutor.com Tactics Manager

Description

1. Player A passes to B1, who checks away from his cone before moving to receive.

2. Player A moves across to receive the pass back (1-2 combination), take a touch and open up his body shape.

3. Player A plays an aerial pass in behind for B2 to run forward onto.

4. Player B2 controls the aerial pass, taking a touch forward and out of his feet.

5. Player B2 either crosses to C who makes a run to the near post, to A who makes a forward run into the centre, or to B1 who makes a run to the far post.

6. Player A, B1 or C try to score. Player A scores in the diagram example.

7. Repeat the sequence on the opposite side: The next Player A plays a 1-2 with B2 and then plays an aerial pass in behind to B1.

Source: Pep Guardiola's Bayern Munich training session at Säbener Strasse Training Ground, Munich - 13th November 2014

119

8. One-Two, Pass Wide, Overlap Run, Cross and Finish

Created using SoccerTutor.com Tactics Manager

Description

1. Player A passes to B.

2. Player A moves off the cone to receive the pass back from B (1-2 combination).

3. Player A passes out wide to C1, who receives on the move

4. Player C1 passes to D, who makes an overlapping run to receive in behind.

5. Player D either crosses to B or C2.

6. Player B or C2 try to score. Player C2 scores in the diagram example.

7. Repeat the sequence on the opposite side: The next Player A plays a 1-2 with B and then passes to C2.

Players A and B switch positions after each sequence. Players C1, C2 and D stay wide.

Source: Pep Guardiola's Bayern Munich training session in Doha, Qatar - 7th January 2014

9. Quick Feet, One-Two and Diagonal Aerial Pass in Behind for Team-mate to Receive and Finish

Created using SoccerTutor.com Tactics Manager

Description

1. Player A takes quick steps towards and back from the pole twice, and then moves forward.

2. The Coach passes to Player A.

3. Player A passes forward to Player C, who drops back with the movement shown.

4. Player C passes the ball back to A.

5. Player A receives, opens up and plays an aerial pass in behind (over the mannequins) for the forward run of Player B.

6. The players rotate positions (A -> B -> C -> A) and the practice continues.

You can run this practice from either side.

Source: Pep Guardiola's Bayern Munich training session at Säbener Strasse Training Ground, Munich

10. Short Combination Play, Pass Out Wide for Cross and Time Runs into the Penalty Area

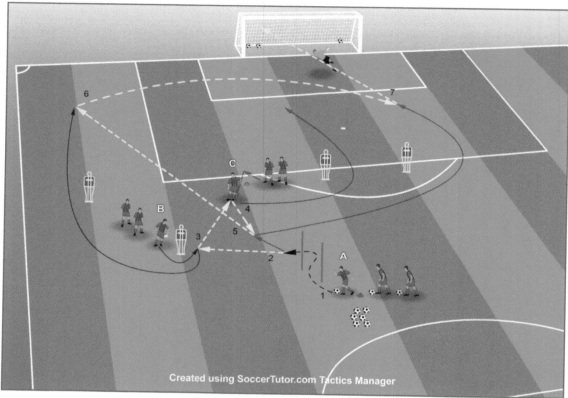

Description

1. Player A dribbles through the poles.

2. Player A passes to B, who drops back and then forward to receive in front of the mannequin.

3. Player B passes to C.

4. Player C plays a lay-off pass back to A.

5. Player A passes out wide and high up the flank for B to run onto after a curved run around the mannequins.

6. Player B crosses into the penalty area.

7. Players A and C both make curved runs around the mannequins and into the penalty area to try and score from the cross. Player A scores in the diagram example.

8. After 4 repetitions each, take 3-4 minutes' rest and then repeat the practice on the right side of the pitch.

Source: Pep Guardiola's training sessions from Barcelona B team (2007-08)

11. Combination with Lay-off, Pass Out Wide for Cross and Time Runs into the Penalty Area

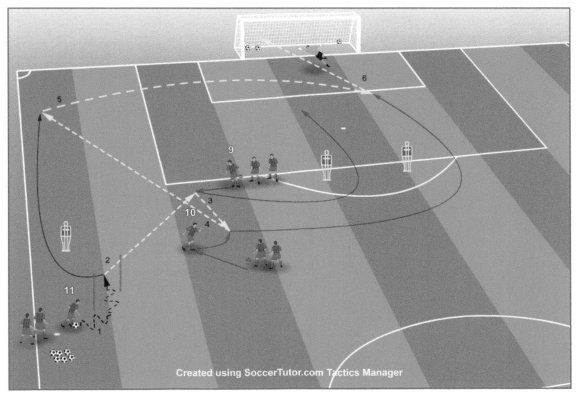

Created using SoccerTutor.com Tactics Manager

Description

1. The left winger (11) dribbles through the poles.

2. The left winger (11) plays a diagonal pass to the forward (9).

3. The forward (9) plays a lay-off pass back to the attacking midfielder (10), who has initially moved diagonally forward and then moves across to receive.

4. The attacking midfielder (10) passes out wide and high up the flank for the left winger (11)

to run onto, after a curved run around the mannequin.

5. The left winger (11) crosses into the box.

6. Both players make curved runs around the mannequins to score: Forward (9) to near post and the attacking midfielder (10) to far post.

7. Players rotate positions (11 -> 9 -> 10 ->11).

8. After 3 repetitions each, take 3-4 minutes' rest and then repeat the practice on the right side of the pitch.

Source: Pep Guardiola's training sessions from Barcelona B team (2007-08)

12. Forward Runs into the Penalty Area, Crossing and Finishing

4 players make runs into the penalty area

All players jog back to their positions (no walking)

Created using SoccerTutor.com Tactics Manager

Description

1. The server (defensive midfielder) passes to the left attacking midfielder, who has dropped back to receive.

2. The attacking midfielder dribbles forward and the left winger makes a forward run.

3. The attacking midfielder passes for the left winger to run onto high up the pitch.

4. The left winger crosses into the penalty area.

5. The 3 attacking players who were waiting on the edge of the penalty area and the right winger have all made forward runs into the penalty area to try and score.

6. All players jog back to their starting positions (no walking) and the practice is repeated with a cross from the right side.

Source: Pep Guardiola's Manchester City training session at Etihad Campus Training Ground, Manchester

13. Short Passing Combination Play On the Flank, Crossing and Finishing

Created using SoccerTutor.com Tactics Manager

The practice runs from both sides of the pitch alternately.

Description

1. Player A passes to B.

2. Player B passes back to A (1-2 combination), who moves across.

3. Player A passes for C to run forward onto.

4. Player C crosses into the penalty area, making sure to evade the 2 mannequins. He can either deliver a high or low cross (cut back).

5. Players D1 and D2 time runs into the penalty area to meet the cross and try to score.

6. If the goalkeeper saves the first attempt, the players should be aware and try to score the rebound.

7. Players A and B rotate positions. The practice is then repeated on the left side.

Source: Pep Guardiola's Manchester City training session at Etihad Campus Training Ground, Manchester - 22nd September 2017

14. Short Passing in the Centre, Play Wide, One-Two, Cut Back and Finish in a 5 v 2 Practice

Created using SoccerTutor.com Tactics Manager

Description

- There are blue 3 players in a central position outside the penalty area and 1 active wide player on each side. There are also 2 red defenders inside the penalty area.

- The practice starts with the Coach's pass and the 3 blue players pass the ball around between themselves, waiting for the right time to play the ball wide.

- After they play a pass wide (either to the left or right), 1 player moves to support the wide

player and the other 2 make runs into the penalty area, as does the other wide player.

- The wide player is put under pressure by the Coach (Pep Guardiola), so plays a 1-2 combination with his team-mate and receives back inside the penalty area.

- From this point, the wide player must deliver the right cross or cut back for a team-mate to score, evading the 2 red defenders.

- The players jog back and the practice restarts.

Source: Pep Guardiola's Manchester City training session at Etihad Campus Training Ground, Manchester - 22nd November 2017

Attacking Combination Play in 3v2 Duels

Direct from
Pep Guardiola's
Bayern Munich
Training Session

1. Fast 3 v 2 (+GK) Duels

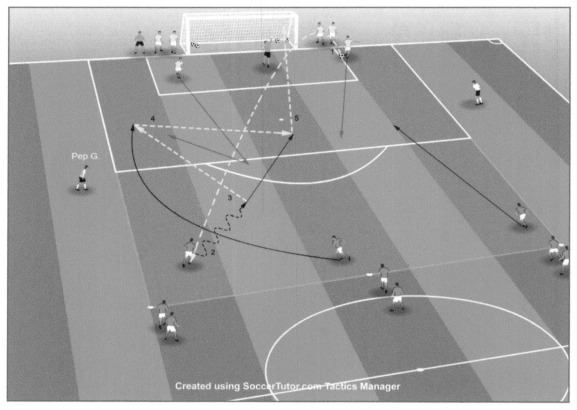

Created using SoccerTutor.com Tactics Manager

Description

- The 3 red players start on the white cones and the 2 yellow players start either side of the goal.

- A yellow player plays an aerial pass to any of the red players.

- The red player who receives dribbles forward to start the attack.

- The aim for the 3 red players is to attack at speed and score as quickly as possible.

- The player that receives dribbles into the centre to occupy the 2 defenders and the other 2 attackers look to receive either side.

- If a wide player receives the aerial pass, the central player makes an overlapping run.

- The first aim is play a well-timed pass to a team-mate in a good position to score.

- A second option is for the player to receive and then deliver a low cross (cut back), as shown in the diagram example.

Source: Pep Guardiola's Bayern Munich training session in Doha, Qatar - 7th January 2014

2. Fast 3 v 2 (+GK) Duels with 1 Defender Starting from a Side Position

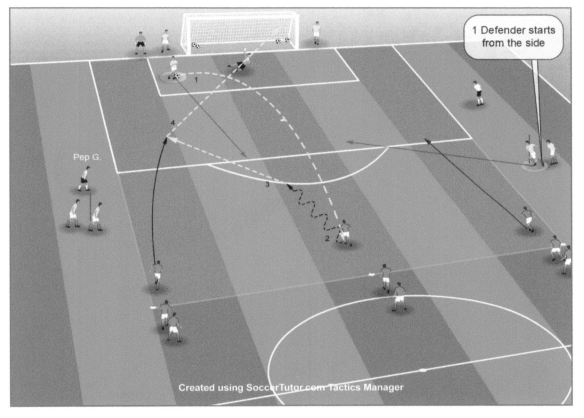

1 Defender starts from the side

Pep G.

Created using SoccerTutor.com Tactics Manager

Description

- This is a variation of the previous practice.

- Now, 1 defender starts from a wide position, rather than next to the goal.

- The red players have to be aware and therefore look to exploit the space on the opposite side to the second defender, as shown in the diagram example.

Source: Pep Guardiola's Bayern Munich training session in Doha, Qatar - 7th January 2014

Attacking Combination Play Circuits

**Direct from
Pep Guardiola's
Bayern Munich
Training Sessions**

1. Combination Play Circuit with Pass in Behind and Finish with Speed Exercises

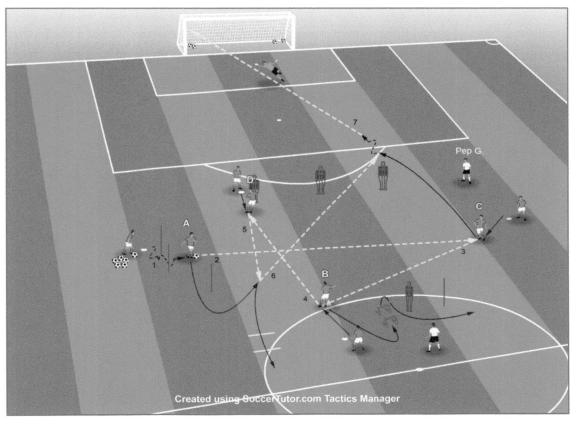

Created using SoccerTutor.com Tactics Manager

Description

1. Player A dribbles through the poles.

2. Player A passes across to Player C. He then runs around the pole.

3. Player C moves off his cone and passes to B.

4. Player B moves off his cone and passes to D. He then jumps over 2 hurdles and runs around the mannequin and pole.

5. Player D passes back to A.

6. Player A passes in between the mannequins and in behind for the run of C. He then skips through the ground poles.

7. Player C controls and shoots (2 touches).

8. The players rotate positions:
   (A -> B -> C -> D -> A).

Source: Pep Guardiola's Bayern Munich training session at Säbener Strasse Training Ground, Munich - 7th January 2016

2. Combination Play Circuit with Diagonal Aerial Pass in Behind and Finish with Speed Exercises

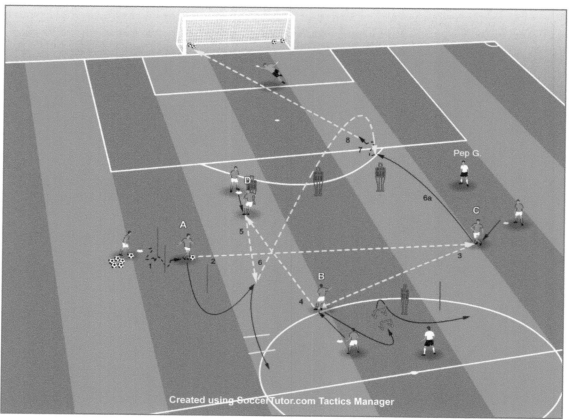

Description

- This is a variation of the previous practice, with just a slight change.

- Player A now plays an aerial pass in behind for C to run onto, control and shoot (2 touches).

Source: Pep Guardiola's Bayern Munich training session at Säbener Strasse Training Ground, Munich - 7th January 2016

3. Combination Play Circuit with Dribbling in Behind and Finish with Speed Exercises

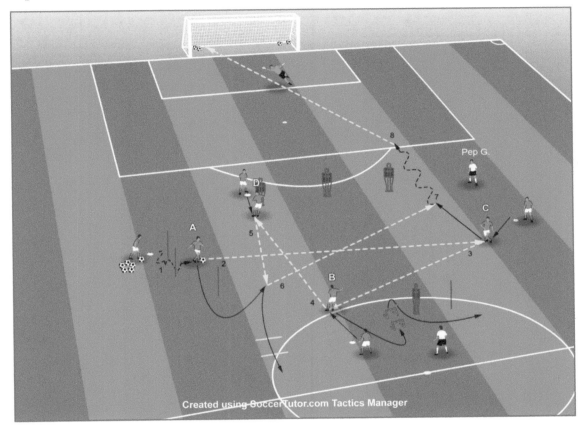

Created using SoccerTutor.com Tactics Manager

Description

- This is a second variation of the previous practices, with just a slight change.

- There is no pass in behind from Player A.

- Player A instead passes across to C in front of the mannequins - Player C receives, dribbles past the mannequin and then shoots to try and score.

Source: Pep Guardiola's Bayern Munich training session at Säbener Strasse Training Ground, Munich - 7th January 2016

4. Passing Circuit with Speed Exercises + Dribble and Finish

Created using SoccerTutor.com Tactics Manager

Description

1. The Coach passes to Player A.

2. Player A passes back to B.

3. Player B receives with an open body shape and takes the ball past the mannequin.

4. Player B passes in between the poles to C, who has jumped over 2 hurdles and moved forward to receive.

5. Player C dribble past the mannequin (simulating 1v1 situation vs defender).

6. Player C shoots at goal.

7. The players rotate positions (A -> B -> C -> A).

Source: Pep Guardiola's Bayern Munich training session at Säbener Strasse Training Ground, Munich

Attacking Combination Play in Conditioning and Speed Practices

Direct from
Pep Guardiola's
FC Barcelona
Training Sessions

1. Passing, Dribbling and Shooting in a Warm-up Circuit

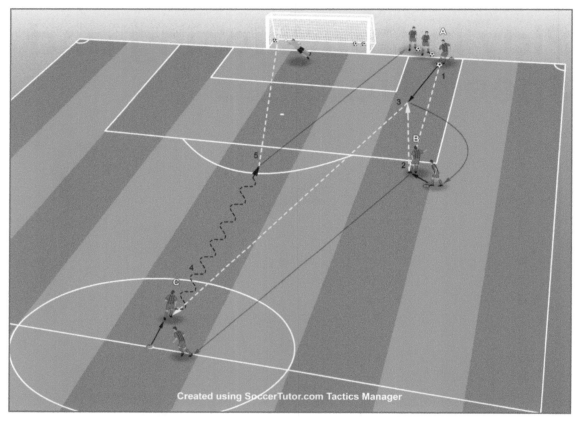

Created using SoccerTutor.com Tactics Manager

The players have 3 minutes of activation and 3 minutes stretching before performing 3 repetitions of this warm-up circuit.

Description

1. Player A passes to B.

2. Player A moves forward to receive the return pass from B (1-2 combination).

3. Player A plays a long pass to C.

4. Player C moves off the cone to receive the long pass and dribbles forward towards the goal.

5. Player C shoots from outside the penalty area.

6. The players rotate positions (A -> B -> C -> A) and the practice continues.

Source: Pep Guardiola's training sessions from Barcelona B team (2007-08)

2. Passing Combination Play with Double One-Two and Shooting in a Warm-up Circuit

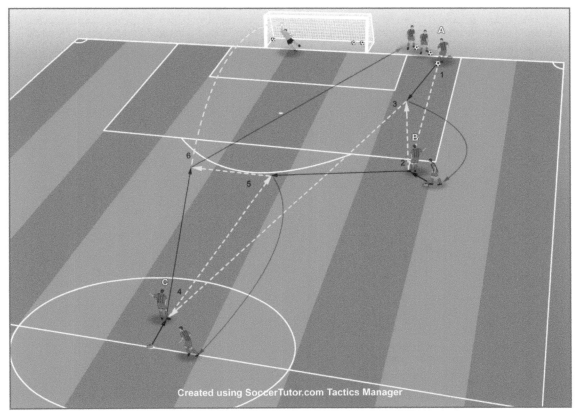

Created using SoccerTutor.com Tactics Manager

The players perform 3 repetitions of this variation and continuation of the warm-up circuit shown on the previous page.

Description

1. Player A passes to B.

2. Player A moves forward to receive the return pass from B (1-2 combination).

3. Player A plays a long pass to C.

4. Player C moves off the cone to receive the long pass and passes into the centre for B to move across and receive.

5. Player B passes the ball for C to run forward onto.

6. Player C shoots from outside the penalty area.

7. The players rotate positions (A -> B -> C -> A) and the practice continues.

Source: Pep Guardiola's training sessions from Barcelona B team (2007-08)

3. Double One-Two Combination, Cross and Finish in a Speed Practice

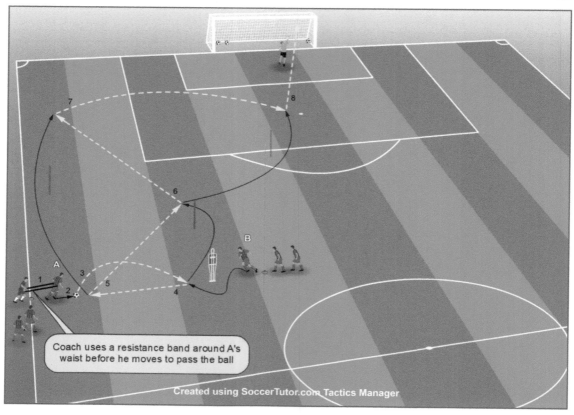

Coach uses a resistance band around A's waist before he moves to pass the ball

Created using SoccerTutor.com Tactics Manager

The players perform 3 repetitions on each side of the pitch, with 3-4 minutes' rest in between.

Description

1. The Coach holds Player A back with a resistance band around his waist.

2. Player A moves to meet the ball.

3. Player A plays a chip pass to Player B.

4. Player B drops back and around the mannequin to receive in front of it and pass back to A (1-2 combination).

5. Player A passes to B again, who runs around the pole to receive.

6. Player B passes wide and high up the flank for A's long curved run around the pole.

7. Player A crosses into the penalty area.

8. Player B makes a curved run around the pole into the penalty area and tries to score from the cross.

Source: Pep Guardiola's training sessions from Barcelona B team (2007-08)

4. One-Two Combination Out Wide, Cross and Finish in a Speed and Conditioning Practice

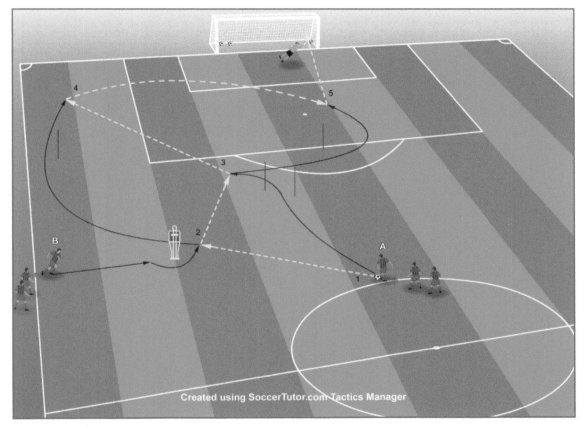

Created using SoccerTutor.com Tactics Manager

The players perform a 1st series of 12 minutes and a 2nd series of 10 minutes, with 2 minutes' rest in between. The aim is a heart rate of 100 bpm.

Description

1. Player B passes to A, who runs inside off the line and around the mannequin to receive.

2. Player B plays a well-timed forward pass to the left of the poles for A to receive after running through them.

3. Player A passes out wide and high up the flank for B to run onto, after a curved run around the pole.

4. Player B crosses into the penalty area.

5. Player A makes a curved run around the pole and into the penalty area to try and score from the cross.

Source: Pep Guardiola's training sessions from Barcelona B team (2007-08)

5. Receiving High Up the Flank to Cross and Timing Runs into the Penalty Area in a Speed Endurance Practice

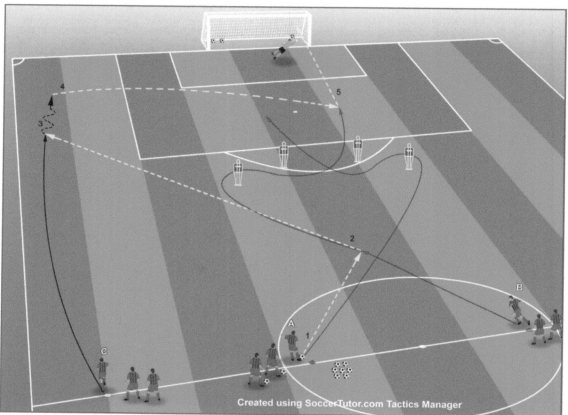

Created using SoccerTutor.com Tactics Manager

The players perform 3 repetitions on each side of the pitch.

Description

1. Player A passes into centre for B to run onto.

2. Player B passes high up the flank for C's forward run.

3. Player C receives and dribbles forward.

4. Player C crosses the ball for his 2 oncoming team-mates (A and B).

5. Both A and B have made curved runs in between the mannequins, then make well-timed cross-over runs into the penalty area to try and score from the cross.

6. The players rotate positions (A -> B -> C -> A) and the practice continues.

7. After 3 repetitions each, repeat with Player C positioned on the right side of the pitch.

Source: Pep Guardiola's training sessions from Barcelona B team (2007-08)

6. Fast Combination Play with Lay-off, Overlap Run, Cross and Finish

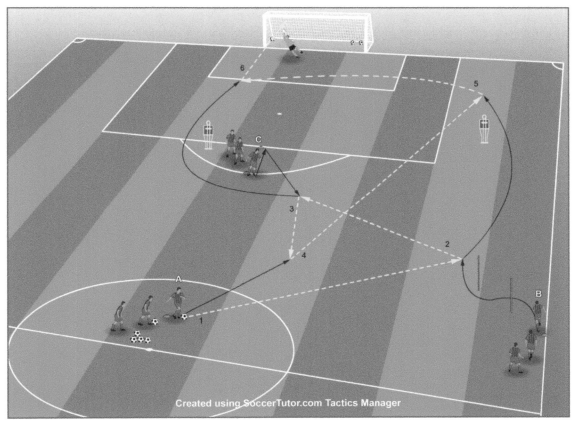

The players perform 3 repetitions on each side of the pitch, with 5 minutes' rest in between.

Description

1. Player A passes across for B to run onto.

2. Player B runs in between the poles to receive and pass to Player C.

3. Player C moves forward and then drops back to receive, before passing back to A.

4. Player A passes out wide and high up the flank for the forward run of B (around the mannequin).

5. Player B crosses the ball for the run of C, who makes a curved run around the mannequin and into the penalty area.

6. Player C tries to score from the cross.

7. The players rotate positions (A -> B -> C -> A) and the practice continues.

Source: Pep Guardiola's training sessions from Barcelona B team (2007-08)

7. Combined Actions, Cross and Finish in a Speed and Conditioning Practice

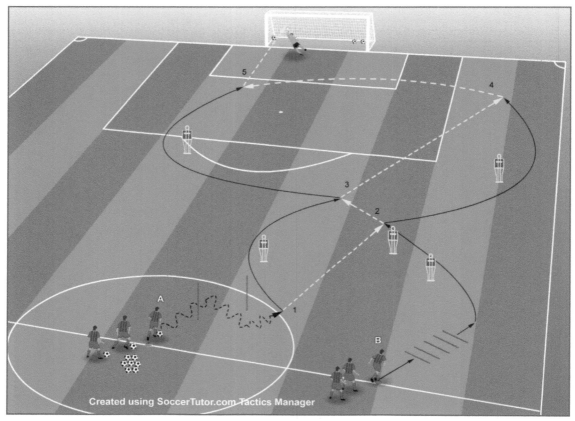

The players perform a 1st series of 3 repetitions and a 2nd series of 4 repetitions, with 4 minutes' rest in between.

Description

1. Player A dribbles through the poles and then passes in front of the 2 mannequins to his right. Player B receives the pass on the move after skipping through the ground poles and running around the 2 mannequins.

2. Player B plays a short pass for A, who receives after a curved run around a mannequin.

3. Player A passes out wide for B, who runs around a mannequin to receive high up.

4. Player B crosses into the penalty area for the well-timed run of A (around the mannequin).

5. Player A tries to score from the cross.

Source: Pep Guardiola's training sessions from Barcelona B team (2007-08)

8. One-Two Combination, Overlap Run for Cross & Time Runs into the Penalty Area in a Speed Endurance Practice

Runs from both sides

Created using SoccerTutor.com Tactics Manager

The players perform 3 repetitions on each side of the pitch, with 3-4 minutes' rest in between.

Description

1. Player A passes forward to B, who moves inside off the line to receive.

2. Player B passes to C, who moves off the cone to receive.

3. Player C passes wide and high up the flank for A's long curved run around the mannequin.

4. Player A crosses the ball for his 2 oncoming team-mates (B and C), who both make curved runs around the mannequins to the far post and into the centre respectively.

5. Either Player B or C try to score from the cross.

6. The players rotate positions (A -> B -> C -> A).

7. Repeat the practice on the opposite side.

Source: Pep Guardiola's training sessions from Barcelona B team (2007-08)

Football Coaching Specialists Since 2001

PEP GUARDIOLA

**Technical Speed
Circuits, Passing,
Rondos, Possession,
SSG's Direct from
Pep's Training Sessions**

Vol. 2

Lightning Source UK Ltd.
Milton Keynes UK
UKHW050820150720
366571UK00003B/20